BRUCE WEBER

SCHOLASTIC BOOK SERVICES
New York Toronto London Auckland Sydney Tokyo

Material for *All-Pro Baseball Stars 1980* closed on
December 20, 1979.

The Author would like to express thanks to the American and
National League public relations offices and the major-league
team publicists for their help in assembling the material for this
book.

Cover photo: Focus on Sports

ISBN 0-590-31537-4

12 11 10 9 8 7 6 5 4 3 2 1   3   0 1 2 3 4 5/8

Printed in the U.S.A.   06

CONTENTS

American League
All-Stars
1979

1B:	Cecil Cooper
2B:	Bobby Grich
SS:	Roy Smalley
3B:	George Brett
OF:	Don Baylor
OF:	Fred Lynn
OF:	Jim Rice
C:	Brian Downing
P:	Mike Flanagan
P:	Ron Guidry

The Orioles' star lefty Mike Flanagan turned a 23-9 season and a 3.08 earned run average into an easy-as-pie Cy Young Award.

First Base
CECIL COOPER
MILWAUKEE BREWERS

Cecil Cooper had one fine 1979. The smooth-fielding first-sacker of the Milwaukee Brewers helped the club to its best season ever (95-66, second in the AL East) with a .308 batting average, 44 doubles (tied for tops in the AL with Chicago's Chet Lemon), 106 runs batted in and 182 hits (both eighth in the league), and 300 total bases (seventh in the AL). Cecil, an ex-Boston Red Sox, was also the Brewers' Mr. Clutch, with 16 game-winning runs batted in. Only Texas' Buddy Bell did as well; no one did better!

So, was the rangy 6-2, 190-pounder happy with his performance? He certainly wasn't.

"It was a good year," he says, "but not a great one. I would have liked a higher batting average. I would have liked to steal more bases (he had 15). And I would have liked more homers. I had 24 with a two-month dry spell and without really shooting for the long ball."

Milwaukee manager George Bamberger thinks all of Cecil's goals are possible. "He's a beautiful player. At the plate, he's a natural. A .330 or .340 batting average? Why not?"

In his three Milwaukee seasons since coming over from Boston, Cooper has never been under .300.

Cecil's only other 1979 disappointment was the team's finish. "You can't be happy with second place," he says. "The pennant. That's our goal for 1980."

A batting title would be pure gravy!

Second Base
BOBBY GRICH
CALIFORNIA ANGELS

Ask any player how he expects to do and he'll tell you, "Great. Just great." That's what Bobby Grich was saying before the 1979 season. But following a back operation and a .251 batting mark in 1978, even Bobby wasn't really sure.

Forget it. For Grich, the California Angels' 31-year-old second-sacker, 1979 was outstanding. It brought him a .294 average, 30 homers, 101 runs batted in, his fourth berth on the American League All-Star Team, and, along with his teammates, a division title.

The RBI total is one of the most impressive stats of Grich's great season. Batting eighth most of the time, the 6-2, 190-pounder had to make the most of his opportunities — and he usually did!

Grich's No. 1 rooter is his long-time teammate (and American League MVP), Don Baylor. "What a comeback," says Baylor, who came up with Grich in the Baltimore organization. "Everyone had written Bobby off. But Bobby didn't — and I didn't. I knew the kind of job he could do. And I knew how determined he was to make it back to the top."

One of Grich's off-season secrets: weight lifting. The nephew of a one-time Olympic lifter, Bobby worked out almost daily before the 1979 season. The hard work paid off.

Any disappointments in '79? Just one. Bob's Angels lost to his old team, the Orioles, in the league championship series. Grich's mission in 1980 is righting that wrong!

5

Shortstop
ROY SMALLEY
MINNESOTA TWINS

"On the whole," says Minnesota manager Gene Mauch, "Roy Smalley is the

6

finest shortstop in baseball." Forget that Smalley is Mauch's shortstop. Forget even that Mauch is Smalley's uncle. The man has a good point.

Though fans of National League All-Pro Dave Concepcion and others may argue, Smalley is right there with the best. Offensively, Roy is solid. His .271 average in '79 was more than respectable, especially when you consider that Smalley was a .230 hitter not long ago.

Few shortstops match his power (24 homers in '79, 19 the year before). The switch-hitting Smalley is most consistent. Last year he hit .271 from the left side of the plate, .270 from the right.

Smalley, the son of 11-year major league shortstop Roy Smalley, Sr., does a fine job in the field. The rangy 6-1, 190-pounder covers lots of ground and throws extremely well. He's sturdy, too. He was the only Twin to play in all 162 games in 1979.

"My dad never really pushed me," says the Twin star. "But he did help me a lot. He taught me how to switch hit. He said it would really help if I wanted to become a ballplayer. And he was right."

Is it difficult to play for your uncle? "Not really," says Smalley. "There's probably as much pressure on him as there is on me. Right after I got to Minnesota, I wasn't doing well. Some people wondered if I'd be playing if I wasn't the manager's nephew. I'm glad he stuck with me. Uncle or not, he's a great manager."

Great managers, of course, love great shortstops!

Third Base

GEORGE BRETT

Kansas City Royals

8

Forgive the folks in Kansas City. So they're a little spoiled. So they can't understand why their darling Royals can't win the AL West title every year.

Sorry, Kaycee fans. Maybe the Angels were three games better in 1979. But they didn't have anything like your man at third, George Brett.

At age 26 (he'll be 27 in May), the 6-0, 200-pounder has established himself as *the* third-sacker in the AL. Even a preseason thumb operation couldn't prevent George from enjoying one of his finest seasons.

Brett, the younger brother of pitcher Ken Brett, is disappointed that he lost the AL batting title to Fred Lynn by four points. But the lefty-swinger's numbers were still impressive. The .329 bat mark included a major-league-leading 212 hits, 85 of them for extra bases. George's 20 three-base hits also led the majors; his 42 doubles tied for third in the AL. And he had 23 homers.

Only four players in this *century* have managed at least 20 doubles, 20 triples, and 20 homers in one season. The last was Hall of Famer Willie Mays — way back in 1957! That's quite a year for Brett.

His only 1979 weakness: his fielding. "The bum thumb was responsible," says ex-Royal field boss Whitey Herzog. "Early in the season, George had no feeling in his thumb. That's when he made most of his errors."

Herzog is one of Brett's biggest fans. "Sure I'll miss him," he says. "The guy loves to play this game — and he plays it so well. That's the perfect combination!"

DON BAYLOR
CALIFORNIA ANGELS

There are baseball players fans love to
watch. And there are players other

players love to watch. The second kind, the players' player, is Don Baylor. He plays the game like it should be played — hard! He plays opening day like he plays in July like he plays in October. Every game is the World Series to Don Baylor.

The 30-year-old former Baltimore Oriole and Oakland A had the season of his life in leading the Angels to the AL West title in '79. In winning Most Valuable Player honors, tough Don hit .296, knocked in 139 runs (to lead the majors), and scored 120 runs (again tops in the big-time).

Only a mid-season injury, which led to an 0-for-27 streak at bat, kept Don from hitting .300 or from cracking the 40-homer barrier (he had 36). He even stole 22 bases.

One problem for Baylor is his streakiness. He can get red hot — which means he can also get ice cold. To make it big, he just has to be hot more than cold — like in '79. That's one reason why his teammates call him "Groove." When Don's in the groove, no one is better.

In addition, no one is tougher. Opposing second basemen and shortstops hate to see Baylor perched on first. Double plays against the Angels are poison to the 6-1, 195-pound Baylor.

Don has a great relationship with his manager, Jim Fregosi. "He's one of the few managers who's been totally honest with me," says Baylor. "I respect him."

Fregosi also respects Baylor. A fine hitter, a man who plays every day, a team leader. What's not to respect?

Outfield
FRED LYNN
BOSTON RED SOX

Like Rodney Dangerfield, Fred Lynn gets no respect. The American League's batting champ isn't even the most talked about Red Sox. He has to battle slugging Jim Rice and veteran Carl Yastrzemski for the affection of Boston's fans. In fact, when the Bosox started looking for pitching help during the off-season, the rumor mills said: Lynn for arms! See, no respect.

The 28-year-old lefty is an outstanding athlete. A one-time Southern Cal football scholarship winner, Lynn won the American League's Rookie of the Year and Most Valuable Player awards in his first season (1975). Except for an injury-plagued 1977 (he hit .260), Fred has been a model of consistency.

His .333 average (and first AL bat crown) was achieved with 177 hits in 147 games, 42 doubles (tied for third in the AL), 39 home runs (tied with Rice for second in the league), and 122 runs batted in (fourth in the AL). He even won a Gold Glove award.

The halfback-sized (6-1, 190 pounds) Lynn thinks he had his best season ever because of his off-season weight training. "It did three things," says Fred. "It made me stronger and a better hitter. It made me tougher for the season's long grind. And it helped protect me against injury."

If Lynn isn't the most popular Red Sox, he takes it pretty hard. "I don't like taking the blame all the time. This is a team game and the team wins or loses together."

The man with the .309 lifetime average is a winner.

JIM RICE
BOSTON RED SOX

Jim Rice was the American League's Most Valuable Player in 1978. He was not in 1979. An off-year? Hardly. Few players have enjoyed a season as good as Rice did in '79. But his Boston Red Sox didn't win any awards for '79 — and neither did Rice.

Jim's most satisfying moment? His 200th hit. (He finished with 201.) That gave him three straight 200-hit seasons. That tied the Boston club record. Was it held by the immortal Ted Williams? No. Rice tied his batting coach, Johnny Pesky.

The powerful 6-2, 205-pounder — who was built to play in Fenway Park — hit a personal-high .325, fourth in the American League, behind teammate and friendly rival Fred Lynn. Not the best in the field, Rice is an artist at bat.

The 27-year-old Rice lost his two-time American League home-run crown to Gorman Thomas of Milwaukee. Still he banged 39 round-trippers, which tied him with Lynn for second in the league. He also scored 117 runs (third in the AL), smacked 39 doubles (seventh), and knocked in 130 runs (second). That gave Jim a two-year total of 269 ribbies and 583 for his five big-league seasons.

Some of the Boston press aren't particularly thrilled with Rice. They have a point. He is kind of quiet. He prefers to let his bat do his talking. And that suits his manager, Don Zimmer, just fine!

Catcher
BRIAN DOWNING
CALIFORNIA ANGELS

16

Pop into Brian Downing's backyard and you'll think you're at spring training. You'll find all the trappings of a big-league camp: a batting cage, weight-training machines, etc. They're all part of Downing's road to No. 1.

A 150-pound "weakling" in high school, the 29-year-old Downing is now a powerful 190 pounds. And he hasn't stopped developing yet.

Brian, who came up with the Chicago White Sox, must be doing something right. After several seasons on the brink of stardom, he blossomed in 1979, just in time to help Gene Autry's Californians to the AL West title. You might expect Boston's Fred Lynn to lead the loop in hitting with .333 or Kansas City's George Brett to finish second with .329. But Brian Downing with .326 for third? You'd have to be dreaming.

No dream. The smooth-fielding Angel backstop found himself at the plate, banging out 166 hits, including 27 doubles, three triples, and 12 homers. His 75 RBIs weren't quite in teammate Don Baylor's class (139), but they helped in the team's flag drive.

Downing's hit mark, best by an AL right-handed hitter in '79 and second-highest in Angel history, came as a total shock to most experts. Brian was a .246 career hitter before last season. Downing couldn't have picked a better time to bloom. He was in the option year of his California contract. His reward: a five-year, $1.8 million contract ($360,000 per year, from 1979 through 1983). Not bad for a former 150-pound weakling!

MIKE FLANAGAN
BALTIMORE ORIOLES

There must be something in the Baltimore air that breeds great pitchers. The Orioles have a long history of top mound men. And now, just as Jim Palmer appears to have run his course, in walks Mike Flanagan, ready to wear manager Earl Weaver's hill crown.

There may have been some doubt about last year's American League Rookie of the Year and National League Most Valuable Player, but there was never a question about the AL Cy Young Award winner. Flanagan, the Birds' 6-0, 195-pound lefty, had it neatly tucked away six weeks before the end of the '79 season. Mike's sparkling 23-9 mark gave the 28-year-old his first 20-win season in only his third full big-league year.

Flanagan, who owns one of baseball's best breaking balls, came close the year before. "I was 12-5 at the All-Star break," he recalls. "It was going to be easy." Then a sore left ankle flared up. Mike went 7-10 the rest of the way and finished 19-15. In '79, with the Birds rolling to the American League flag, Mike again had 12 wins at All-Star time, then rang up 11 more. Over his three full seasons, Mike has won 57 games. Among American Leaguers, only the Yanks' Ron Guidry (59) has won more.

The reasons for your success, Mike? "My slider and change-up. Before this, all I had were my fastball and curve. If the fastball wasn't hopping or the curve wasn't breaking, I was out of luck. Variety — that's what's doing it for me!"

RON GUIDRY
NEW YORK YANKEES

Let's say you're a Yankee fan. You've
been out of the country for a couple of

20

years. No TV, no radio, no newspapers. A friend hands you the 1979 Yankee statistics. You glance down the list to pitchers.

"Hmmm," you say. "Look at this Ron Guidry. Some season. Won 18, lost only eight. Wow! A 2.78 earned run average. Best in the American League! Great. And 201 strikeouts. The second straight year over 200. No other Yankee pitcher has ever done that. A super year!"

You'd be right, of course. For any mere human, 18-8, 2.78 ERA, 201 strikeouts, 15 complete games (eighth best in the league), and a .692 winning percentage would be a fine season. But somehow Yankee fans expected more. It's unfair.

The 5-11, 162-pound Guidry, small by big-league fireballer standards, had one of baseball's all-time great seasons in '78. So when he slipped to human level — and the Yankees slipped to fourth place in the AL East — people started asking questions. Not to worry, as they say. There's nothing wrong with Guidry that a healthy reliever Goose Gossage might not have helped. That was the New Yorkers biggest problem. When the starter couldn't finish — as Guidry couldn't in 18 of his 33 starts — there was no one to pick him up.

Still, we'll call Ron's 1979 season — only his fourth in the big-leagues — outstanding. In addition to the won-lost and ERA figures, he also rang up a 13-strikeout performance against Detroit last May and won 11 straight games between July 21 and September 21. We should all have "off-seasons" like that one.

National League
All-Stars
1979

1B: **Keith Hernandez**
2B: **Davey Lopes**
SS: **Dave Concepcion**
3B: **Mike Schmidt**
OF: **Dave Kingman**
OF: **Dave Parker**
OF: **Dave Winfield**
 C: **Ted Simmons**
 P: **J. R. Richard**
 P: **Bruce Sutter**

Forty-five homers, 114 runs batted in, a .565 slugging
average, and a Gold Glove: Phillie 3B Mike Schmidt had
everything in '79 — except a National League pennant.

First Base
KEITH HERNANDEZ
ST. LOUIS CARDINALS

Okay, Willie Stargell fans, calm down. No doubt about it. Your man Pops had one great season, particularly at playoff and World Series time. He may have been the Most Valuable Player in the National League. But the No. 1 first baseman had to be Keith Hernandez.

The 26-year-old St. Louis first-sacker did everything a player could do in 1979. His .344 batting average was tops in the majors. So was his total of 48 doubles. He scored 116 runs to lead the National League and banged out 210 hits, second only to teammate Garry Templeton. He smacked 11 triples and banged in 105 runs, trailing only established sluggers like Dave Winfield, Dave Kingman, Mike Schmidt, and Steve Garvey. That's some company.

Better still was Keith's glove work. His superb play in the field — only six errors all season — won him a Gold Glove, not easy when a Steve Garvey plays the same position.

The Cards waited years for Hernandez. His .255 batting average in 1978 convinced some of the doubters that Keith would never make it. The 6-0, 185-pounder from San Francisco was the talk of the Card camp as long ago as 1972.

"Lou Brock really helped me," said the league's co-MVP (with Stargell). "He taught me that there would be good times and bad times and that I couldn't let myself go too far either way."

Maybe that doesn't explain a 89-point increase in Hernandez's batting average. But it isn't bad advice.

Second Base
DAVEY LOPES
LOS ANGELES DODGERS

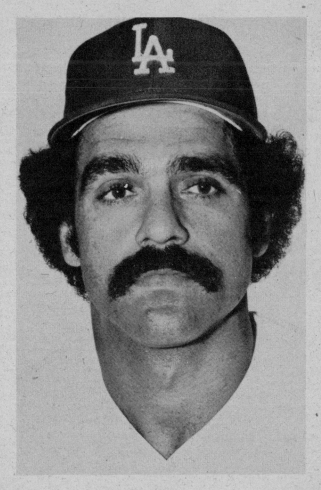

Why would you take an All-Pro second baseman and make him your center fielder? Because you want to win a pennant.

That's the L.A. Dodgers' idea in proposing the switch of their second-sacker, 33-year-old (34 in May) Davey Lopes, to the middle of their outfield. (Lopes wasn't entirely opposed to the idea, but he wanted extra pay to make the change.)

Dodger manager Tom Lasorda felt that Lopes in center might allow him to get more punch into the L.A. lineup. It isn't surprising. Little Davey has become a slugger in his "old" age. Following a career-high 17 home runs in 1978, Lopes blasted 28 four-baggers in '79.

How does a singles-hitter who makes his living as a base-stealer (Lopes had 44 swipes in '79) become a slugger?

"I don't really know," says the 5-9, 175-pounder. "I'm not really swinging that much harder. I am trying for a more level swing. Maybe it's the ball. It just seems to jump off the bat. I'm just waiting for my pitch and smashing it when I get it."

Though Lopes' average was only .265 last year, he still did the job as the Dodger lead-off hitter. In addition to 154 hits, he walked 97 times, scored 109 runs, and batted in 73. Not bad output.

"My secret," says Lopes, "is really no secret. I'm learning. I'm a smarter player. And I'm getting more respect from the opponents' pitchers."

Second base or center field, this little David is a giant.

DAVE CONCEPCION
CINCINNATI REDS

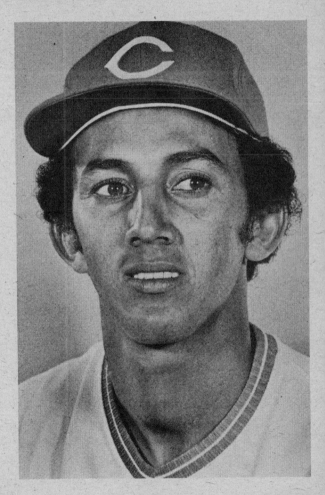

There are lots of nuts and bolts in the Big Red Machine. But the main cog? That could be shortstop Dave Concepcion. You may hear more about George Foster or Tom Seaver or even slumping Johnny Bench. But year in and year out, it's Concepcion, the pro at bat and in the field.

His glove work is well known. The 1979 Gold Glove was almost taken for granted. It was the 6-1, 180-pounder's fifth in the last six years. Other shortstops may be smoother or quicker or have better arms. But absolutely no one in either league does everything as well as Concepcion.

The 31-year-old from Venezuela does pretty well with the bat, too, though his average slipped from .301 in 1978 to .281 in 1979. Still, no one expected Dave to be a factor at the plate when he broke in. His 1971 average? Only .205.

Concepcion's 1978 performance was a key to the Reds' NL West title. Long-time Reds Tony Perez and Pete Rose were making their living in Montreal and Philadelphia, respectively. But it was the Reds who were making it to the league championship series.

Rookie manager John McNamara was one of those who was duly impressed with his shortstop. "We had a very young infield, especially with Joe Morgan's disappointing year. But the glue, day in and day out, was Concepcion. He's beautiful."

Like two well-tuned racehorses,
Chicago's Dave Kingman and Philly's
30

Mike Schmidt played Longball Derby through the summer. And though Kingman won the homer battle, 48 to 45, Mike's output certainly qualified him as the NL's No. 1 third baseman.

For Schmidt, it was a year to remember — following a year to forget. In 1978, the second year of a $550,000 per year contract, Mike was horrid. His homer total: a mere 21. His batting average: only .251. Injuries put him on the shelf for three weeks. It was the pits.

Though the average didn't improve much in '79, the rest of the numbers did. In addition to his club-record homers, he led the league with 20-gamers (game-winning hits) and 120 walks. He became the first Philly in 20 years to homer in every stadium. And when Wally Post did it in 1959, there were only eight NL parks. (Now there are 12!)

It was hard to top Mike's July. He hit .354 with 16 homers (seven in five games) to take Player of the Month honors.

Another National League Gold Glove award was the icing on top of Mike's delicious 1979 cake.

"The big thing is that I stayed healthy last season," says the solid 6-2, 203-pounder. "I'm not really disappointed about losing the homer race. Kingman has a lot of advantages. Wrigley Field (Dave's home park) is an easier home-run park — the wind often blows out, they only play during the day. Sometimes I'm a little jealous."

A Philly return to the top of the NL East this year would relieve any pain.

Outfield
DAVE KINGMAN
CHICAGO CUBS

They ought to post a warning sign on Chicago's Waveland Ave., just beyond the left-field wall at Wrigley Field. Walking there can be extremely dangerous during Cubs' games. You never know when Dave Kingman is liable to deposit a "bomb" on the block.

At 6-6 and 210 pounds, the Chicago left-fielder is super-strong. During a national TV game last season, Dave was badly fooled by San Diego pitcher Bob Owchinko. Lunging across the plate, Dave swiped at the ball with his right hand entirely off the bat. Somehow he made contact, hit the ball to straight-away center, the deepest part of the park, and watched it sail over the wall for one of his major-league-leading 48 homers. (He also had 115 RBIs and 16 game-winning hits, third in the league.)

After bouncing from the Giants to the Mets to the Padres to the Yankees, Kong seems to have found a home with the Cubs. Wrigley Field is tailor-made for the slugger who first made news at Southern Cal. But Dave grew up in the suburbs of Chicago. "I used to come to the park to watch Ernie Banks and Billy Williams," he remembers.

The 31-year-old isn't the best gloveman in the league, though he's surprisingly fast and throws well. But he doesn't make his living with his glove — and his bat work was never better than in '79.

First, Dave hit .288; that's 56 points higher than his lifetime average.

Second, he has learned to do things at the plate — hit to right, hit more grounders — that are destined to make him a much better hitter.

Kingman is a private person. Besides baseball, the two things he loves most are fishing and being left alone. He's pretty quiet — until he gets a bat in his hands!

DAVE PARKER
PITTSBURGH PIRATES

You may not remember an old TV series called *The Millionaire*. They're replaying it in Pittsburgh these days. Only this time the star is a sleek 6-5, 230-pound baseball machine named Dave Parker.

The Pirates' Six Million Dollar Man (a million a year for six years) played second-fiddle to Willie Stargell in the world-champs' publicity league. But he was second to no one on the field.

Despite nearly constant pain in his left knee for the last couple of months of the season, Dave had a banner year. He hit .310 for the season with a respectable 25 homers and 94 runs batted in.

As the weather got colder, Dave's bat got hotter. In the league playoffs against Cincinnati, he hit .333, including a game-winning 10th-inning single in Game 2. In the World Series against Baltimore, Dave soared to .345, his sore knee and a pair of unreal fielding plays by Baltimore third baseman Doug DeCinces notwithstanding.

Though the soon-to-be 29-year-old Parker's stats for 1979 were impressive, some experts felt he could have done even better. Dave has set some pretty tough standards for himself. His fielding — he was a Gold Glove winner in '77 and '78 — slipped a bit in '79 and that disturbed him.

Still, Dave has set his sights for 1980 on winning the triple crown (batting, home run, and RBI titles). Though the home-run crown seems out of reach as long as Dave Kingman is healthy, Parker is capable of anything.

"If Dave stays healthy," says Buc manager Chuck Tanner, "and if he's allowed to keep his mind on baseball, there's no telling how far he can go. He's just a super athlete!"

DAVE WINFIELD
SAN DIEGO PADRES

The head man at the David M. Winfield Foundation in San Diego is quite a guy. He spends thousands of dollars every year doing good things for children. On the side, he also plays a little baseball for the San Diego Padres.

Third in the National League's Most Valuable Player voting (the highest finish ever by a Padre), Winfield enjoyed a great 1979 — on and off the field.

On the field, he hit .308 (eighth in the league), banged 34 homers (third), had 16 game-winning hits (tied for third), smacked 10 triples (seventh), and knocked in a league-leading 118 runs. Only Mike Schmidt received more votes in the NL All-Star team voting by the fans.

In one game (at Atlanta last July 31), the former U. of Minnesota basketball star went 5-for-5, including a double, a homer, and a walk. He scored four runs and drove in four. He also had one four-hit game, 13 three-hit games, and 27 two-hit games.

Dave's Winfield Foundation distributed free tickets to games in San Diego, Los Angeles, and New York, held a party for 5,000 youngsters at the Seattle All-Star Game, and conducts a scholarship program in St. Paul, Minnesota.

"I didn't have any money when I was a kid," says Winfield. "A lot of people helped me get where I am today. And this is just one way I can do something positive. Other athletes are helping me in this work and so are the people who are making contributions to the Foundation."

Dave's an All-Pro in any league!

TED SIMMONS
ST. LOUIS CARDINALS

How important is Ted Simmons to the St. Louis Cardinals? Try these numbers on for size. When a broken left wrist kept Ted on the sidelines for 28 games last July, St. Louis won 11 games but lost 17. That's six games under .500. For the season, the practically re-born Redbirds were 10 games over .500. Were it not for Ted's injury, St. Loo might have been in the thick of the NL East title fight.

It took a long time, but now everyone knows that Ted Simmons is Mr. Big among National League catchers. Used to be that Johnny Bench was the only name you'd ever hear. With Bench having his problems, Bob Boone not quite at Simmons' level, and Gary Carter, Ed Ott, and John Stearns still coming on, switch-hitting Simmons is the leading backstop, year in and year out.

Unfortunately, the wrist injury took its toll on Simmons' season. From a .321 pre-injury average, he slumped to .283 (.274 righty, .291 lefty). But any season, however short, that includes 26 homers and 87 RBIs isn't bad. Ted was one big reason why St. Louis led the National League in hitting with a rousing .278 mark.

The sturdy 6-0, 200-pounder is only 30. That leaves him plenty of time to reach one of his primary individual objectives: 35 homers in a season. The Cards' Busch Stadium isn't home-run paradise. But Ted is sure he can make it. Can he? He has done everything else he has put his mind to!

Pitcher
J. R. RICHARD
HOUSTON ASTROS

The Los Angeles Dodgers aren't too fond of James Rodney Richard. To put it mildly, the Astros' basketball-player-sized fireballing right-hander owns L.A. The

Dodgers haven't beaten him since June 1976. The streak is now 11 straight.

The rest of the National League isn't doing much better. J. R., the huge 6-8, 237-pounder, struck out 313 opponents in 1979, best in the majors, and rolled up a league-leading 2.71 ERA. Though his season record was only 18-13, J. R. went 4-1 (with a 1.24 ERA) during Houston's fruitless run at the NL West pennant in September. That won him Pitcher of the Month honors.

The Astros hope that the late-season Richard manages to find his way back to the Houston camp this season. J. R. had a 7-11 record as late as last July 20. From then on he zoomed to 11-2. One of the losses was a 1-0 squeaker in Philadelphia.

Richard's teammates have a word for his pitching: "mean." They say he really hates opposing batters. They also say that he's the best pitcher in baseball. That's something that James Rodney will have to prove with a completely overpowering season.

"Even when J. R. was losing early in the season," recalls Astro boss Bill Virdon, "he was pitching well. He'd have one bad inning and that would be it. Late in the season, he managed to avoid the bad inning."

Control used to be a Richard problem. But no more. His ratio of 9.65 strikeouts to 3.02 walks per nine innings was just what the doctor ordered. Now, with fastballing Nolan Ryan joining Richard on the Houston staff, the opponents may be ordering the doctor.

BRUCE SUTTER

CHICAGO CUBS

42

Relief pitchers have it pretty easy. It's late in the game. The hitters have been at it in the broiling sun all day. In walks the man with the fresh arm, ready to buzz unhittable fastballs, big-bending curves, super sliders.

And then there's Bruce Sutter. He's Chicago's main man in the bullpen. There's no one better in baseball at what Bruce does. Opponents have been known to moan out loud when the rugged 6-2, 190-pounder takes over for Chicago.

Want to hear Cy Young Award-winning numbers? Bruce pitched in 62 games, winning six while losing six, and saving a league-record tying 37. That means he had a hand in 43 of the Cubbies' 80 wins. That's 54% of all the victories. No National League pitcher with 100 or more innings had a lower earned run average (2.23).

The Sutter secret? Batters say it's his special split-fingered fastball. The thumb, Sutter reports, is the secret. "I use it all the time," he says. "It gives me extra speed and it helps the ball break better." The batters say it acts like a spitball in the way it breaks, down and away.

One of Sutter's problems is energy. He seems to run out of gas in September every year. "It's tough to throw as hard as I do," he says, "and keep up the pace. One of the reasons for my success in '79 was Dick Tidrow. His arrival took some of the pressure off me." (Tidrow actually made more appearances than Sutter, 65-62.) "Two innings at a time," says 27-year-old Bruce. "That's perfect."

COVER STORY

First Baseman
PETE ROSE
PHILADELPHIA PHILLIES

Pete Rose didn't win any awards last season. At best, he was the No. 3 first-baseman in the National League, behind co-MVPs Keith Hernandez of St. Louis and Pops Stargell of Pittsburgh. But he *was* voted Player of the Decade by *The Sporting News* and *Baseball Magazine*.

But he's on the cover of *All-Pro Baseball Stars 1980*, and he deserves it. When Philly owner Ruly Carpenter made Pete a rich man (3.2 million bucks for four years) at age 38, experts wondered about Ruly's sanity. He turned out to be crazy, of course, just like a fox. What did old Pete do to earn his daily bread? He played in all 163 Phillie games (including a tie) to lead the club. He hit .331, second best in the National League (behind Hernandez), and his top performance since a .338 year in 1973.

Did the "old" guy tire as the season dragged on? No way. He was at his best in September, hitting an incredible .421 for the month to win NL Player of the Month honors. A 23-game hitting streak, longest in the majors in 1979, won him the Aqua Velva award, started by the company after Pete's 44-game streak in 1978. In all, Pete hit safely in 26 of his last 27 games.

That helped the Phils go 18-11 for the month, good enough to sew up the manager's job for interim boss Dallas Green. And he stole 20 bases, a career high!

But better than all of that were Pete's two all-time records. His 200th hit gave him his 10th 200-hit season. The old mark, nine, was held by the immortal Ty Cobb.

And Pete's 2,427th single on August 5 gave him the all-time NL singles record. The previous record-holder: Honus Wagner.

Love him or hate him, the Player of the Decade is unbelieveable!

ALL-PRO ROOKIES
1979
AMERICAN LEAGUE

Third Baseman

JOHN CASTINO
MINNESOTA TWINS

At 5-11 and 175, he's one of the smallest
Twins . . . but the 25-year-old swung a hot
bat as a freshman, with a .285 hit mark in
148 games . . . already on the way to be-
coming fine glove man at hot corner . . . a
future Gold Glover . . . was ticketed for
minors last spring but made big jump from
Class AA to big-time . . . injury to vet Mike
Cubbage gave Castino the job full-time
. . . shared Rookie Award with Toronto's
Alfredo Griffin.

Shortstop

ALFREDO GRIFFIN
TORONTO BLUE JAYS

At age 22 last season, Alfredo was
youngest of AL's crop of super rookies . . .
shared Rookie Award with Castino, beat-
ing out New York pitcher Ron Davis,
Chicago pitcher Ross Baumgarten,
California hurler Mark Clear, and Texas'
1B Pat Putnam . . . hit .287 with 179 hits
and 31 RBIs in 153 games . . . native of
Dominican Republic . . . still lives there
. . . switch-hitter made former Jay SS Luis
Gomez available for trade . . . AL Player of
the Month for September when he hit more
than .400.

46

NATIONAL LEAGUE

Pitcher
RICK SUTCLIFFE
LOS ANGELES DODGERS

Dodgers' 23-year-old right-hander was easy winner in Rookie Award voting . . . was team's top winner (17-10) with a 3.46 ERA . . . won nine of his last 11 decisions, including one stretch of six in a row . . . his two post-All Star losses were by 2-1 and 3-2, two of his six one-run losses . . . got first chance to start on May 3 when Burt Hooton got flu . . . pitched complete game and remained a starter all season . . . good hitter (.247, 17 RBIs, one homer).

Outfielder
SCOT THOMPSON
CHICAGO CUBS

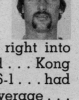

Lanky 6-3, 175-pounder fits right into Cubs' basketball-sized outfield . . . Kong Kingman is 6-6, Jerry Martin is 6-1 . . . had 100 hits in 346 at bats for .289 average . . . 24-year-old is Cubs' man from Mars . . . he lives in Mars, PA . . . played in 128 games . . . Houston's switch-hitting Jeff Leonard was other outstanding NL outfielder with .290 bat mark.

AMERICAN LEAGUE
1979 STANDINGS

East

	Won	Lost	Pct.	GB
Baltimore	102	57	.642	—
Milwaukee	95	66	.590	8
Boston	91	69	.569	11½
New York	89	71	.556	13½
Detroit	85	76	.528	18
Cleveland	81	80	.503	22
Toronto	53	109	.327	50½

West

	Won	Lost	Pct.	GB
California	88	74	.543	—
Kansas City	85	77	.525	3
Texas	83	79	.512	5
Minnesota	82	80	.506	6
Chicago	73	87	.456	14
Seattle	67	95	.414	21
Oakland	54	108	.333	34

and Previews for 1980

Ken Singleton

AL East
BALTIMORE ORIOLES

The 1979 Orioles won 108 games and lost only 62. It was one win too few, one loss too many. The Birds have spent the winter wondering how they blew a 3-1 lead in the '79 World Series and figuring how they can reverse that result in '80.

The cast, led by brainy manager Earl Weaver, is basically the same, including hard-hitting, switch-hitting OF Ken Singleton (.295 overall, .313 lefty), hard-hitting, switch-hitting 1B Eddie Murray (.295 overall), OF Al Bumbry (.285), and DH Lee May (.254).

Singleton was the power (and the glory) for the '79 Birds with 35 homers and 111 RBIs to go with his other numbers.

3B Doug DeCinces, possibly Howard Cosell's favorite Oriole, was bothered by back pain and hit only .230. SS Mark Belanger, blessed with a fine glove, was a disaster at the plate (.167). Kiko Garcia (.247) and Rich Dauer (.257) shore up the infield, and C Rick Dempsey (.239) is adequate. His back-up, Dave Skaggs (.248), had off-season back surgery and is a question mark.

The pitching staff, led by unhappy Jim Palmer (10-6) and Cy Young Award winner Mike Flanagan (23-9), is an Oriole strength. Scott McGregor (13-6), Steve Stone (11-7), and Dennis Martinez (15-16) are the other top starters.

Mike Caldwell

AL East
MILWAUKEE BREWERS

The Brewers' best season ever came up eight games short last year. Their 95-66 record, good enough to win the Western Division easily, was only second best in the Eastern Division. The Orioles were just that good!

Manager George Bamberger is certain that the same players who came close in '79 can go all the way in '80. Though Milwaukee looked for help during the off-season, the Brewers came up empty.

The outfield is a strong point. Despite (ugh!) 175 strikeouts, chunky Gorman Thomas (.244) set club records with 45 homers (tops in the AL), 123 RBIs, and 98 walks. Sixto Lezcano (.321) had a .573 slugging percentage, third in the league.

First-baseman Cecil Cooper (.308) topped his 44 double-106 RBI season with a Gold Glove. 2B Paul Molitor hit .322 (sixth in the league), banged 16 triples, and stole 33 bases.

Led by lefty Mike Caldwell (16-6 despite a pulled rib muscle), the Brewer pitchers did well in '79 (the league's fourth best ERA). Though the relievers amassed only 23 saves, the starters completed 61 games, tops in the majors. Jim Slaton (15-9) and Lary Sorenson (15-14) were other mainstays among the starters.

Dennis Eckersley

AL East
BOSTON RED SOX

The Red Sox's 1980 pennant hopes are "battery operated." Improved pitching and catching — that's baseball's battery — are the keys to Boston's drive to overtake Baltimore, Milwaukee, New York, or whomever in the AL East.

The Sox have plenty of offensive firepower. Any club that has outfielders Jim Rice and Fred Lynn playing side-by-side should. Rice hit .325 with 39 homers and a stunning 130 RBIs in '79. Lynn chipped in with a .333 hit mark and 122 RBIs, while also stroking 39 homers. Even old 1B Carl Yastrzemski (he'll be 41 in August) was super — with a .270 average, 21 homers, and 87 RBIs in 147 games. Overall, Boston hit .283, tops in the majors.

Shortstop Rick Burleson (.278) had a good, if not great, season. But 3B Butch Hobson (.261) was hurting all season. Boston will miss DH Bob Watson (.337 in 84 games), gone to the hated Yankees. OF Dwight Evans (.274) is solid.

Catching is one major problem. Pudge Fisk (.272 but only 91 games) never seems to be 100% healthy. Last year it was a sore elbow. Gary Allenson, who replaced Fisk, hit only .203 in 108 games.

Pitching is in worse shape. The Sox's high 4.03 ERA was their undoing. Righty Dennis Eckersley (17-10, 2.99 ERA) was the staff leader.

AL East
NEW YORK YANKEES

What do you do if your world champions slip to fourth place? If you're Yankee owner George Steinbrenner, you clean house — completely!

George's youth movement, which starts with new 42-year-old manager Dick Howser, includes both trade prizes and free agents. The Yanks hope that 25-year-old Rick Cerone (.239 with Toronto) can replace the late Thurman Munson.

Power-hitting Jim Spencer (.288, 23 homers) is the #1 first-sacker, now that Chris Chambliss is gone. The rest of the infield, 2B Willie Randolph (.270), SS Bucky Dent (.230), and 3B Graig Nettles (.253), is back, though there were doubts about Dent and Nettles last season. 3B Eric Soderholm (.272 with Texas) and powerful 1B-DH Bob Watson (.337 in 84 games with Boston) are the new additions.

New York hopes ex-Mariner 25-year-old Ruppert Jones (.267) can firm up the outfield. He stole 33 bases for Seattle last year. OFs Reggie Jackson and Lou Piniella, both of whom hit .297 in '79, are better at bat than in the field.

Ex-Blue Jay lefty Tom Underwood (9-16, 3.69 ERA) and rookie lefty Dave Righetti join a mound staff that includes biggie lefties Tommy John (21-9) and Ron Guidry (18-8), and righties Ron Davis (14-2) and Luis Tiant (13-8).

Steve Kemp

AL East
DETROIT TIGERS

Manager Sparky Anderson is accustomed to spending October at the World Series. And 1979 was no exception. Unfortunately, Sparky was there as a broadcaster, not a manager, a situation he'd like to correct in 1980.

There's a chance, of course, but not a great one. Detroit's 85-76 record was good, but not nearly good enough to catch Baltimore.

Detroit welcomes ex-Expo reliever Dan Schatzeder and his 10-5 record. But Tiger fans are angry that the team had to give up exciting OF Ron LeFlore, his .300 batting mark, 180 hits, and 78 steals. Bad deal!

OF Steve Kemp (.318, 105 RBIs, and 26 homers) swings a mighty bat, as do Champ Summers (.313 and 20 homers in 90 games) and Jason Thompson (.246 and 20 homers). Ex-Pirate, Philly, and Met IF Richie Hebner, off a disappointing season in New York, should bounce back.

If the question-mark arms ever come around, Detroit will win the AL title. Milt Wilcox (12-10), Jack Billingham (10-7), and reliever Aurelio Lopez (10-5) are the solid vets. The youngsters, like Dan Petry (6-5), solid Jack Morris (17-7), and Pat Underwood, (6-4 after a 6-0 start) are coming. John Hiller? Mark Fidrych?

Rookies to watch: OF Kirk Gibson, OF Dave Stegman, P Mike Chris.

53

Andre Thornton

AL East
CLEVELAND INDIANS

The Indians aren't thrilled with geography — the geography that put them in the AL's Eastern Division. They'd prefer to be in the softer West.

For 1980, manager Dave Garcia, in his first full season, starts without pitcher Rick Wise (15-10, 3.73 ERA), gone to San Diego as a free agent, and outfielder Bobby Bonds (.275, 25 homers, 85 RBIs, 34 steals), gone to St. Louis (he wanted too much money). The Bonds deal brought pitcher John Denny and outfielder Jerry Mumphrey.

That starts Cleveland a little short for the new decade. Indian management paid big bucks to keep 1B Mike Hargrove (.325 and 56 RBIs in 100 games). Improved Del Alston (.290 in 54 big-league games) joins Jim Norris (.246) and Rick Manning (.259) in the outfield.

Cleveland's Mr. Clutch, huge ex-Yank C-DH Cliff Johnson, hit .271 and smacked a team-leading nine game-winning hits after coming from New York. Duane Kuiper (.255), Toby Harrah (.279), and Tom Veryzer (.220) are adequate if not steady. Powerful Andre Thornton (.233) hit 26 homers despite a sore shoulder.

Pitching, despite Sid Monge's 12-10, 2.40 ERA, and Rick Waits' 16-13, 4.44 ERA, could be better.

54

John Mayberry

AL East
TORONTO
BLUE JAYS

The oldest rookie of all time? Could be
Bob Mattick. At age 64, he's the new manager of the Blue Jays.

The team drew 1.4 million fans at home
in '79. If Toronto (53-109 last year) ever gets
decent, there's no telling how many will
show up.

Management is trying. There will be
lots of new Jays in '80, including a whole
bunch of ex-Yankees and ex-Braves. Key
man in all the moves is former New York
1B Chris Chambliss. He came to Toronto
with a pair of fine rookies, IF Damaso Garcia and P Paul Mirabella.

Chambliss didn't last long in Toronto.
The Jays moved him along to Atlanta,
along with former starting SS Luis Gomez,
for RHP Joey McLaughlin, OF Barry Bonnell, and SS Pat Rockett.

Righty McLaughlin, 5-3 and a 2.48 ERA
in half a season with Atlanta, was the key
to deal #2. But Bonnell (.259 and 12 homers
as a part-timer) could be an important factor.

The newcomers aren't alone. There's
other talent in Toronto, including big 1B
John Mayberry (.274 and 21 homers), top
rookie SS Alfredo Griffin (a switch-hitter
who hit .287), and OF Al Woods (.278). The
pitching staff is a disaster (4.81 ERA
in '79).

Rod Carew

AL West
CALIFORNIA ANGELS

Can the Angels do it again? They're going to have to do it without fireballer Nolan Ryan (16-14, 223 strikeouts) and 1B Willie Mays Aikens (.280, 81 RBIs).

But they overcame lots of stumbling blocks to take the AL West title in '79. For instance, 1B Rod Carew missed 52 games with a bum thumb and tonsillitis. He hit a "human" .318, not even as much as surprising catcher Brian Downing. The 29-year-old backstop smacked the ball at a .326 pace, 80 points over his lifetime mark.

Don Baylor, the AL's most valuable player, spent the off-season begging for a raise. Did he deserve it? Perhaps. He led the majors in RBIs (139), broke club records in runs (120) and total bases (333), hit .296, and banged 36 homers while playing in all 162 games. All-star 2B Bobby Grich had a great year (30 homers, 101 RBIs, .294 average). OF Dan Ford (.290) had off-season knee surgery. 3B Carney Lansford (.287) is only 23 and could be the Angel third-sacker for years.

Pitching could be a question mark, especially without Ryan. Lefty Frank Tanana got into only 18 games in '79 with a 7-5, 3.89 ERA mark. Second-year man Mark Clear tries to improve on his 11-5 and 14-save mark. Dave Frost (16-10, 3.57) is solid.

AL West
KANSAS CITY ROYALS

Whitey Herzog learned baseball's most famous lesson the hard way. After winning three straight AL West titles, manager Herzog let the Royals slip to second.

His replacement, Jim Frey, a long-time Oriole coach, has the personnel to return the Royals to the top. They don't come any better than his All-Pro 3B George Brett (.329, 23 homers, 107 RBIs). They don't come any quicker than OF Willie Wilson, who matched a switch-hitting .315 average to his 83 (of 95) stolen bases. OF Amos Otis comes off another fine season (.295, 90 RBIs, 30 steals).

The Royals will miss OF Al Cowens (.295, 73 RBIs), gone to California for powerful 1B Willie Mays Aikens (.280, 21 homers), who fills a big Kaycee hole. C Darrell Porter (.291) is one of the AL's best, at bat and with the glove. Lefty-swinger Pete LaCock, son of TV's Peter Marshall, will back up Aikens and serve as a part-time DH. With Fred Patek (.252) gone to California as a free agent, U. L. Washington (.254) becomes the #1 shortstop for now. 2B Frank White (.266) is solid.

The starting pitchers are fine, though they could have done better in '79. Dennis Leonard (14-12), Paul Splittorff (15-17), Larry Gura (13-12), and Rich Gale (9-10) can win pennants. The bullpen, with 9-4 Al Hrabosky gone, needs help.

Jim Sundberg

AL West
TEXAS RANGERS

Texas Ranger owner Brad Corbett spent a fairly quiet off-season. He did some of his wheeling and dealing during the 1979 season (a third-place, 83-79 year), picking up ex-Yankee centerfielder Mickey Rivers, ex-Met first-sacker Willie Montanez (.319 with Texas), and ex-A's pitcher John Henry Johnson (2-6 as a Ranger). They didn't help.

For 1980, Montanez may move to the outfield, joining Rivers (.293) and Al Oliver (.324). Gold Glove 3B Buddy Bell had an outstanding 1979, with a .299 average, 18 homers, 101 RBIs, 200 hits, 42 doubles, and a league-leading (tied) 16 game-winning hits. The rest of the infield was a problem. Young SS Nelson Norman, who became a switch-hitter at mid-season (.222), showed a leaky glove. 2B Bump Wills (.273) was just fair.

C Jim Sundberg (.275) is just about the top Ranger. In addition to his work at the plate, Jim won his fourth straight Gold Glove in '79.

Relief P Jim Kern (13-5, 29 saves) was the AL's top fireman. Texas might have pulled out the flag had lefty Jon Matlack (5-4) been healthy.

The Rangers have the offensive firepower to win, but the pitching must be more consistent, and the team must avoid cold spells like last summer's 10-30 streak!

Jerry Koosman

AL West
MINNESOTA TWINS

People who listen to Howard Cosell are convinced that Oriole manager Earl Weaver is baseball's #1 genius. But people who know think that no one is ahead of Minnesota's Gene Mauch.

Somehow, he manages to win (82-80) with the players given to him by penny-pinching Cal Griffith.

In 1980, he'll have to do without P Dave Goltz, a 14-game winner in 1979 and a 20-game winner in 1977. But 1979 20-game-winner lefty Jerry Koosman (20-13, 3.38 ERA) is back, along with bullpen ace Mike Marshall (10-15, 2.64 ERA, 32 saves of the club's total of 33). Lefty Geoff Zahn was 13-7 a year ago, with a 3.57 ERA.

Elsewhere, Minny has lots of options. C Butch Wynegar (.270, 57 RBIs) is solid, as is All-Pro SS Roy Smalley (.271, 24 homers, 25 RBIs). 1B Ron Jackson (.271) will get plenty of work, though part-time 3B Mike Cubbage (.276) may get some action at first, too. Rookie-of-the-Year 3B John Castino hit .285 and is set at third. Regular 2B Rob Wilfong sparkled in '79 with a .313 mark. The infield is solid.

There's plenty of outfield firepower too, with Ken Landreaux (.305 in '79), Bombo Rivera (.281), Hosken Powell (.293), and Dave Edwards (.249).

Rookies to watch: OF Gary Ward, P Wally Sarmiento.

Lamar Johnson

AL West
CHICAGO
WHITE SOX

Chisox manager Tony LaRussa is a lawyer. But his baseball problems — and there are many — don't require legal aid.

First, the 73-89 Sox start the new decade a little weaker than they finished the last. C Milt May (.254) and IF Jorge Orta (.262) have left through the free-agent door. P Francisco Barrios (8-3, 3.61 ERA) underwent off-season arm surgery. When he'll be back is anyone's guess. Barrios is the team's only proven right-handed pitcher.

The lefty moundmen aren't bad. Ross Baumgarten (age 24) went 13-8 with a 3.54 ERA. Rich Wortham (age 26) went 14-14 with a 4.90 ERA. Steve Trout, son of onetime big-league-hurler Dizzy Trout, is 22 and had an 11-8 mark (3.89 ERA) last season. The old man, 28-year-old Ken Kravec, was 15-13 and 3.74. Righty Ed Farmer (3-7 but 14 saves) is the main man in the bullpen.

Mike Colbern (.241), Marvis Foley (.247), and newcomer Bruce Kimm will battle for the catching spot vacated by Bill Nahorodny (gone to Atlanta).

LaRussa has some decent offense (the team hit .275 last year). OF Chet Lemon (.318, 86 RBIs) is just a peg below All-Pro. He can do it all. IFs Alan Bannister (.285) and Lamar Johnson (.309) are pros. Jim Morrison (.275) did well in his 67 Chicago games in '79.

60

Bruce Bochte

AL West
SEATTLE
MARINERS

The Mariners are progressing. Their 1979 edition finished 67-95 — not great, it's true. But it was 13 games better than division rival Oakland and 14 better than fellow expansionist Toronto.

Manager Darrell Johnson will have a bunch of new faces to work with in 1980, any of whom might lift the M's.

Speedy Juan Beniquez, far better than his .254 mark in 62 games for the Yankees last year, replaced Ruppert Jones (who goes to New York). Ex-Yank organization pitcher Rick Anderson (13-3, a 1.63 ERA at Columbus, OH) could be the key.

Onetime Indian 3B-OF Ted Cox joins the battle for the Seattle third-base job with Danny Meyer (.278) and Bill Stein (.248 with injuries). Mario Mendoza, a good-glove, no-hit (.198) man tries to hold onto his shortstop position against ex-Angel Jimmy Anderson. All-Star Bruce Bochte (.316, 16 homers, 100 RBIs) is set at first.

The M's hope that switch-hitting Rodney Craig (a .315 hitter in the minors) can move up full-time in 1980. If so, he'll join Beniquez and Leon Roberts (.271), Tom Paciorek (.287), and Joe Simpson (.283) in the outfield.

Dave Revering

AL West
THE A's

It matters not where the A's play. In Denver or Oakland, they're awful. Their 54-108 record was just a hair better than Toronto's. And the A's were world champs as recently as 1974.

Star 1B-DH Dave Revering had 14 homers and 43 RBIs in the last half of the season while hitting nearly .300. Still, the full-season numbers — .288, 19 homers, 77 RBIs — were nothing to write home about.

Shortstop Rob Picciolo hit only .253, but that beat his lifetime mark by 40 points. Pitcher Rick Langford bounced back from a 1-9 start to finish with a 12-16 record, not bad on a 54-108 club.

It takes some terrible years by better players to produce the A's kind of record. Take OF Mitchell Page. The onetime All-Rookie star hit only .247, with nine homers and 42 RBIs.

SS Mario Guerrero played only 46 games — his teammates questioned whether he was really hurt — and hit only .229. Onetime Giant relief-star Dave Heaverlo went 4-11 with a 4.11 ERA and nine saves, but pitched very little the second half of the season. Young righty P Steve McCatty did well (11-12) after coming up from Ogden.

Rookies to watch: P Jeff Jones, OF Ray Cosey.

62

NATIONAL LEAGUE
1979 STANDINGS

East

	Won	Lost	Pct.	GB
Pittsburgh	98	64	.605	—
Montreal	95	65	.594	2
St. Louis	86	76	.531	12
Philadelphia	84	78	.519	14
Chicago	80	82	.494	18
New York	63	99	.389	35

West

	Won	Lost	Pct.	GB
Cincinnati	90	71	.559	—
Houston	89	73	.549	1½
Los Angeles	79	83	.488	11½
San Francisco	71	91	.438	19½
San Diego	68	93	.422	22
Atlanta	66	94	.413	23½

and Previews for 1980

Omar Moreno

PITTSBURGH PIRATES

Like Cinderella, the Pirates spent most of the winter pinching themselves. They wanted to make sure that their miracle win over the Orioles wasn't a dream.

Well, fellas, it wasn't, and with any kind of luck (and some pitching help), you could do it again in October 1980.

It'll take some doing, of course. Onetime starting 2B Rennie Stennett is gone. SS Tim Foli (.291 with Pittsburgh) will have to do as well again. But Bill Madlock (.298 overall, .328 with the Pirates) should do at least as well. The man is some hitter.

Rightfielder Dave Parker (.310) has had even better years than in 1979. When he's hot, there's no one better. But the big man for the Pirates in '79 was 1B Wilver (Willie) Stargell. Old Pops, the 1979 co-MVP of the National League and solo MVP of the World Series, hit .281 with 32 homers and 82 runs batted in. Not bad, especially for someone who turned 39 in March.

The pitching staff, led by Bert Blyleven (12-5) and gutty lefty John Candelaria (14-9), is adequate, but not great. It will miss Bruce Kison (13-7), who left for California. If Don Robinson (8-8) and Rick Rhoden are healthy, the Pirates' chances will soar.

How do the Pirates spell relief? T-E-K-U-L-V-E, of course. Kent (10-8) is the strongest string bean in the game!

Gary Carter

MONTREAL EXPOS

Montreal fans are convinced that their Expos clinched the 1980 National League pennant the day they pried Ron LeFlore loose from Detroit.

The speedy LeFlore surely won't hurt. A .300 hitter for three of the last four seasons, Ron stole 243 bases during the same period. He should move to leftfield for Montreal, with solid Andre Dawson (.275, 92 RBIs) in center.

LeFlore cost Montreal ace relief-pitcher Dan Schatzeder (10-5). The Expos also lost infielder Tony Perez (.270) to the Red Sox and pitcher Rudy May (10-3) to the Yankees as free agents. Part-time infielder Dave Cash (.321 in 76 games) brought IF Bill Almon and OF Dan Briggs from San Diego.

The new additions strengthen the Montreal outfield, where Ellis Valentine (.276) should join LeFlore and Dawson. Flashy Rodney Scott (.238, 39 steals) is set at second with ex-outfielder Warren Cromartie (.275) an early choice at first. Expo MVP Larry Parrish (.307, 30 homers, 82 RBIs) is the third baseman. Young vet Gary Carter (.283) is the catcher.

Without May and Schatzeder, pitching could be a problem. But there's solid young talent, like Steve Rogers (13-12 and 30 years old) and David Palmer (10-2 and only 22 years old).

Garry Templeton

NL East
ST. LOUIS
CARDINALS

The surprise team of the NL East a year ago, the Cards hope they've filled in enough holes to make a real run at the title.

The club's basic lineup is solid. Co-MVP Keith Hernandez had the kind of season most players only dream about. The 26-year-old hit .344 with 105 RBIs and won a Gold Glove. Shortstop Garry Templeton, only 24 years old, battled Cincinnati's Dave Concepcion for top-shortstop honors. Garry hit .314 with 211 hits and 19 triples, the last two figures the NL's best.

The hot-hitting Cards (their .278 team average was tops in the league) have lots of other firepower, including veteran outfielder George Hendrick (.300), thirdsacker Ken Rietz (.268), second-baseman Ken Oberkfell (.301), and All-Star catcher Ted Simmons (.283).

St. Louis manager Ken Boyer apparently wasn't satisfied, because the Cards hit the trade market for often-troublesome outfielder Bobby Bonds. (.275 with 25 homers and 85 RBIs for the Indians last year).

Pitching is the only St. Louis problem, though there's hope for continued good performances from righties John Fulgham (10-6) and Silvio Martinez (15-8). Mark Littell (9-4, 2.19 ERA) is solid in the bullpen.

NL East
PHILADELPHIA PHILLIES

It's hard to believe that the Phillies weren't better than they were in '79.

It's up to the new manager, Dallas Green, to put the pieces back together for the 1976, '77, and '78 NL East champs. There's lots of raw material. Ageless Pete Rose (.331) stole a career-high 20 bases and hit .421 in September as the NL's Player of the Month.

Third-sacker Mike Schmidt is the NL's best at his position. Mike batted only .253, but smacked 45 homers and knocked in 114 runs. He also drew 120 walks, tops in the National League.

There's no question that Phils can hit the ball. The team batting average in '79 was .266. Leftfielder Greg Luzinski (.252, 81 RBIs) should improve. Catcher Bob Boone (.286) is solid offensively and defensively. Outfielder Bake McBride (.280, 25 steals) was on the Philly trading block most of the winter.

The Phillies' major problem: pitching, particularly in the bullpen. Lefty Steve Carlton (18-11) was among the best in the NL. But his 3.62 ERA could have been better. Nino Espinosa (14-12, 3.65 ERA) didn't scare anyone, nor did Barry Lerch (10-13, 3.74), or reliever Ron Reed (13-8, but 4.15).

Rookies to watch: RHP Marty Bystrom. RHP Scott Munninghoff.

Rick Reuschel

NL East
CHICAGO CUBS

For a fifth-place ball club, the Cubs played pretty exciting baseball in 1979. But they still finished fifth. And for a fifth-place ball club, they didn't do much to improve themselves for '80.

There may not have been much of a reason to. The team hit .269, led by leftfielder Dave Kingman. Slugging Kong, the 31-year-old strongman, smacked a league-leading 48 homers (second best in Cub history), banged 19 doubles and five triples, and hit .288. Quite a year!

Offensively, Kingman had plenty of help. First-baseman Bill Buckner (.284) had 14 game-winning hits, only two fewer than team-leader Kingman. The rest of the infielders, including young vet Ivan De Jesus (.283) and Steve Ontiveros (.285), are okay.

Despite a rotten September, which saw his average sink from .325 to .289, the Cubs' man from Mars (that's Mars, PA), Scot Thompson, was a rookie sensation. Ex-Oakland A Miguel Dilone hit .306 in 43 late-season games, and centerfielder Jerry Martin could improve his .272 mark.

Led by the league's strongest bullpen (Cy Young winner Bruce Sutter and 11-5 Dick Tidrow), the Cub mound staff is strong. Chicago pitchers struck out 993 batters, tops in the NL. Rick Reuschel (18-12) is the best of the starters.

NL East
NEW YORK METS

How sad! The 1969 world champs became the laughing stocks of 1979. Even when they tried to trade top pitcher Craig Swan (14-13) to the California Angels, they couldn't get it right. The owner stopped the deal.

Pros? The Mets have a few. Outfielder Lee Mazzilli (.303, 79 RBIs) is a potential All-Star. A healthy Steve Henderson (.306 in 98 games) makes the outfield even stronger. Shortstop Frank Taveras, who came from Pittsburgh for Tim Foli early last year, hit .263 with 42 steals, the latter a club record. John Stearns (.243) is a fine receiver, but could hit a little more. The best all-around Met may be rightfielder Joel Youngblood, a .275 hitter last year.

The biggest Met weakness is on the mound. Considering some of the pitchers this team once owned (Seaver, Koosman, Ryan), the current staff is the pits. Swan, if he makes it to opening day, is the best the team has. Pat Zachry (5-1 in seven starts before an injury finished him for the season) will help, if he's healthy.

The Mets will miss Skip Lockwood (2-5, but only a 1.50 ERA), gone to Boston as a free agent. Hard-luck Pete Falcone (6-14, 4.16 ERA) could improve. Minor-league Player of the Year Mark Bomback (22-7 at Vancouver) may help.

Tom Seaver

NL West
CINCINNATI REDS

Manager John McNamara did everything anyone expected of him last year — except win the championship series. The rough, tough Cincinnati fans will be expecting that honor this year!

He's going to have to do it with pretty much the same crew he directed last year. While their NL West challengers made wholesale changes, the Reds did little.

Cincinnati owns some fine, young talent. 3B Ray Knight filled Pete Rose's shoes neatly, playing every day and hitting .318, third best (right behind Rose) in the NL. OF Dave Collins played every game after the All-Star break and also hit .318. SS Dave Concepcion (.281) is still going well. But 1B Dan Driessen (.250) had an off-year. C Johnny Bench (.276), now 32, is looking for time off behind the plate. OF Ken Griffey, off a knee operation, hit .316 in 95 games before surgery in '79. George Foster (.302) missed 41 games.

Star right-hander Tom Seaver started slowly in '79 but finished 16-6 with a fine 3.14 ERA. But there's young talent, too, with Mike LaCoss (14-8), Tom Hume (10-9), and Frank Pastore (6-7). Hume and Doug Bair (11-7) run the bullpen. A lefty starter was one of Cincy's top off-season needs.

Rookies to watch: 2B Ron Oester, LHP Charlie Liebrandt.

70

Joe Niekro

NL West
HOUSTON
ASTROS

In 1979, Chicago's Dave Kingman blasted 48 home runs. The 1979 Houston Astros collected only 49 between them. Though Houston enjoyed its best year ever, finishing only 1½ games behind Cincinnati and remaining in the NL West race until two days before the end of the season, lack of power is a real problem.

Houston's strong suit is pitching. Imagine opposing batters — they now have to face fire-balling J. R. Richard and Nolan Ryan, back to back. Ryan (16-14 with California) struck out 223 AL batters in '79. Richard (18-13) led the world with 313 strikeouts.

Just when the enemy focuses in on their smoke, Houston can counter with knuckle-balling Joe Niekro (21-11). By the fourth night, they'll be in shock! Ken Forsch (11-6) gives the Astros great depth. Most experts didn't figure Joaquin Andujar (12-12) to be with the club in '80.

A healthy Cesar Cedeno (.262) would boost Astro hopes. But there's plenty of outfield help with Jose Cruz (.289), Terry Puhl (.287), and Dennis Walling (.327). Elsewhere, Enos Cabell (.272), Art Howe (.248), and catcher Alan Ashby (.202) could do better.

Rookies to watch: OF Danny Heep, C Alan Knicely.

Steve Garvey

NL West
LOS ANGELES DODGERS

Forty-three wins in the last 69 games (a .623 pace) brought the Dodgers' 1979 record to 79-82 and third in the NL West. That would be good for some teams, but not L.A.

What did the team do? It opened up the bank books and brought in right-handed pitchers Dave Goltz from Minnesota and Don (Stan the Man) Stanhouse from Baltimore, and outfielder-first sacker Jay Johnstone from Philadelphia. Dodger manager Tom Lasorda figures that the two arms will bolster his fading mound staff. Goltz should be a starter; Stanhouse may be the first man in from the bullpen.

The signing of Johnstone means that Davey Lopes (.265) will remain at second for L. A. Steve Garvey (.315) closed fast to become only the 16th player ever to get five-straight 200-hit seasons. Little 3B Ron Cey (.281) smacked 28 homers to become the all-time L. A. home-run king. OF Dusty Baker (.274), OF-C Joe Ferguson (.262), and C Steve Yeager (.216) could all do better.

Rookie of the Year P Rick Sutcliffe (17-10, 3.46 ERA) was the Dodgers' top winner, as Don Sutton faded to 12-15 and Burt Hooton to 11-10. The loss of pitchers Andy Messersmith, Doug Rau, Terry Forster, and Bob Welch was too much to overcome.

Rookies to watch: OF Bobby Mitchell, IF Jack Perconte.

Mike Ivie

SAN FRANCISCO GIANTS

The editors of *All-Pro Baseball Stars* are even sorrier than you are about the Giants. We picked them to win last year.

What do the Giants have in store for us this time? It's hard to say. Management tried hard to make some changes. They brought in the limit of free agents — three. All of them are a little flawed.

Ex-Pirate second-baseman Rennie Stennett is only 29, but he may still have problems with a 1977 broken ankle.

Catcher Milt May is 29 and hit .254 with the Tigers and White Sox in '79. But he had shoulder surgery last August.

Ex-Brewer OF Jim Wohlford is 28 and hit .263 last year. He'll battle four or five Giants for the starting left-field job.

Elsewhere, the Giants are expecting much better from unhappy Vida Blue. His 14-14 record accompanied a sky-high 5.01 ERA last year. With 10-9 John Curtis gone to San Diego, the Giants have real problems with their mound staff.

How long can 1B Stretch McCovey (.249) keep it up? He's 42 years old. Mike Ivie (.286, 27 homers, 89 RBIs) is rolling. So are OF Jack Clark (.273, 26 homers) and Bill North (.259). SS Roger Metzger's off-season power-saw accident (he lost four finger-tips) could end his career.

Rookies to watch: P Bill Bordley, OF Chris Bourjos.

NL West
SAN DIEGO PADRES

You can't fault the Padres for not trying. San Diego comes into every season with high hopes, gives just a hint of future success, flops, then rebuilds.

This past winter was no exception. New manager Jerry Coleman (last year's Padre broadcaster) inherits a 68-93 team that probably should have done better. He has superstar Dave Winfield (.308, 34 homers, 118 RBIs, third in the MVP voting). He has some decent pitching, including Randy Jones (11-12, 3.63 ERA) and reliever Rollie Fingers (9-9 and 13 saves). His shortstop, Ozzie Smith, a third-year man, disappointed last year (.211).

Most important, Coleman hopes that some of his new faces can turn the club around. There's fine-fielding 3B Aurelio Rodriguez, a 13-year man who hit .254 in 106 games for the Detroit Tigers last year. There's vet 2B Dave Cash, who lost his job with Montreal last season.

Ex-Indian Rick Wise and ex-Giant John Curtis join Jones, 8-16 lefty Bob Shirley, 6-12 lefty Bob Owchinko, 6-9 righty Eric Rasmussen, and possibly 12-11 righty Gaylord Perry on the San Diego mound crew.

A power-hitting first baseman and a sure-handed centerfielder were also on San Diego's most-wanted list.

Gary Matthews

NL West
ATLANTA BRAVES

The 1979 Braves' year-end report zeroed in on the team's speed (a club-record 98 steals), September play (10-6 in the final weeks), and OF Gary Matthews' fine all-around season. But a 66-94 year is a tough one to overcome.

As you'd expect, the Braves didn't stand still. (They never do.) First they picked up the no-longer terrifying relief-pitcher Al Hrabosky. They got Chicago White Sox catcher Bill Nahorodny.

Then they pulled one of the biggies of the winter meetings by swapping with Toronto for ex-Yankee 1B Chris Chambliss and SS Luis Gomez. They cost Atlanta OF Barry Bonnell (a favorite of Braves' boss Ted Turner), SS Pat Rockett, and pitcher Joey McLaughlin. Chambliss, who never actually played for Toronto, was Atlanta's key man, though Gomez could start.

It's not that the '79 Braves had no talent. Besides Matthews (.304 average, 27 homers, 90 RBIs, 97 runs), the Braves had powerful 3B Bob Horner (.314, 33 homers in 121 games), speedy OF Jerry Royster (.273, 164 hits, 35 steals), and even switch-hitting OF Ed Miller (.310).

Knuckleballing Phil Niekro (21-20) continues to move up on the all-time pitching-records list. Hrabosky joins vet Gene Garber (6-16, but 25 saves) in the Braves' bullpen.

HOW THEY'LL FINISH IN 1980

National League East
1. Montreal Expos
2. Pittsburgh Pirates
3. Philadelphia Phillies
4. St. Louis Cardinals
5. Chicago Cubs
6. New York Mets

National League West
1. Cincinnati Reds
2. Houston Astros
3. San Francisco Giants
4. Los Angeles Dodgers
5. San Diego Padres
6. Atlanta Braves

American League East
1. New York Yankees
2. Baltimore Orioles
3. Milwaukee Brewers
4. Boston Red Sox
5. Detroit Tigers
6. Cleveland Indians
7. Toronto Blue Jays

American League West
1. Kansas City Royals
2. Texas Rangers
3. California Angels
4. Minnesota Twins
5. Chicago White Sox
6. Seattle Mariners
7. The A's

American League Champions: New York Yankees
National League Champions: Cincinnati Reds
World Champions: Yankees

1979 STATISTICS
AMERICAN LEAGUE
Batting
(175 or more at-bats)
*Bats Left-handed †Switch-Hitter

Batter and Club	PCT	G	AB	R	H	HR	RBI	SB
Adams, Glenn, Minn.*	.301	119	326	34	98	8	50	2
Aikens, Willie, Calif.*	.280	116	379	59	106	21	81	1
Ainge, Dan, Tor	.237	87	308	26	73	2	19	1
Alexander, Gary, Clev	.229	110	358	54	82	15	54	4
Allenson, Gary, Bos.	.203	108	241	27	49	3	22	1
Anderson, Jim, Calif.	.248	96	234	33	58	3	23	3
Armas, Tony, Oak.	.248	80	278	29	69	11	34	1
Bailor, Bob, Tor.	.229	130	414	50	95	1	38	14
Bando, Sal, Milw.	.246	130	476	57	117	9	43	2
Bannister, Alan, Chi.	.285	136	506	71	144	2	55	22
Baylor, Don, Calif.	.296	162	628	120	186	36	139	22
Belanger, Mark, Balt.	.167	101	198	28	33	0	9	5
Bell, Kevin, Chi.	.245	70	200	20	49	4	22	2
Bell, Buddy, Tex.	.299	162	670	89	200	18	101	5
Bochte, Bruce, Sea.*	.316	150	554	81	175	16	100	2
Bonds, Bobby, Clev.	.275	146	538	93	148	25	85	34
Bosetti, Rick, Tor.	.260	162	619	59	161	8	65	13
Brett, George, K.C.*	.329	154	645	119	212	23	107	17
Brohamer, Jack, Bos.*	.266	64	192	25	51	1	11	0
Brookens, Tom, Det.	.263	60	190	23	50	4	21	10
Bumbry, Al, Balt.*	.285	148	569	80	162	7	49	37
Burleson, Rick, Bos.	.278	153	627	93	174	5	60	9
Campaneris, Bert, 8-Tex. 85-Calif.	.230	93	248	29	57	0	15	13
Carew, Rod, Calif.*	.318	110	409	78	130	3	44	18
Carty, Rico, Tor.	.256	132	461	48	118	12	55	3
Castino, John, Minn.	.285	148	393	49	112	5	52	5
Cerone, Rick, Tor.	.239	136	469	47	112	7	61	1

Batter, Club	PCT	G	AB	R	H	HR	RBI	SB
Chalk, Dave,								
9-Tex. 66-Oal.	.223	75	220	15	49	2	13	2
Chambliss, Chris, N.Y.* ...	.280	149	554	61	155	18	63	3
Cooper, Cecil, Milw.*	.308	150	590	83	182	24	106	15
Cowens, Al, K.C.	.295	136	516	69	152	9	73	10
Cox, Ted, Clev.	.212	78	189	17	40	4	22	3
Cox, Larry, Sea..........	.215	100	293	32	63	4	36	2
Cruz, Julio, Sea.†	.271	107	414	70	112	1	29	49
Cubbage, Mike, Minn.* ...	.276	94	243	26	67	2	23	1
Dauer, Rich, Balt.	.257	142	479	63	123	9	61	0
Davis, Dick, Milw.	.266	91	335	51	89	12	41	3
DeCinces, Doug, Balt.	.230	120	422	67	97	16	61	5
Dempsey, Rick, Balt.	.239	124	368	48	88	6	41	0
Dent, Bucky, N.Y.	.230	141	431	47	99	2	32	0
Downing, Brian, Calif.	.326	148	509	87	166	12	75	3
Edwards, Dave, Minn.	.249	96	229	42	57	8	35	6
Edwards, Mike, Oak.	.233	122	400	35	93	1	23	10
Ellis, John, Tex..........	.285	111	316	33	90	12	61	2
Essian, Jim, Oak.	.243	98	313	34	76	8	40	0
Evans, Dwight, Bos.	.274	152	489	69	134	21	58	6
Fisk, Carlton, Bos.	.272	91	320	49	87	10	42	3
Ford, Dan, Calif..........	.290	142	569	100	165	21	101	8
Gamble, Oscar,								
64-Tex. 36-N.Y.*	.358	100	274	48	98	19	64	2
Gantner, Jim, Milw.*	.284	70	208	29	59	2	22	3
Garcia, Kiko, Balt.	.247	126	417	54	103	5	24	11
Garr, Ralph,								
102-Chi. 6-Calif.*	.269	108	331	34	89	9	39	2
Grich, Bobby, Calif.	.294	153	534	78	157	30	101	1
Griffin, Alfredo, Tor.†	.287	153	624	81	179	2	31	21
Gross, Wayne, Oak.*	.224	138	442	54	99	14	50	4
Grubb, Johnny, Tex.*	.273	102	289	42	79	10	37	2
Hargrove, Mike, Clev.*	.325	100	338	60	110	10	56	2
Harlow, Larry,								
38-Balt. 62-Calif.*	.240	100	200	27	48	0	15	2
Harrah, Toby, Clev.	.279	149	527	99	147	20	77	20
Hassey, Ron, Clev.*	.287	75	223	20	64	4	32	1
Heath, Mike, Oak.	.256	74	258	19	66	3	27	1
Henderson, Rickey, Oak. ..	.274	89	351	49	96	1	26	33
Hobson, Butch, Bos.	.261	146	528	74	138	28	93	3

Batter, Club	PCT	G	AB	R	H	HR	RBI	SB
Horton, Willie, Sea.	.279	162	646	77	180	29	106	1
Howell, Roy, Tor.*	.247	138	511	60	126	15	72	1
Jackson, Ron, Minn.	.271	159	583	85	158	14	68	3
Jackson, Reggie, N.Y.*	.297	131	465	78	138	29	89	9
Johnson, Lamar, Chi.	.309	133	479	60	148	12	74	8
Johnson, Cliff,								
28-N.Y. 72-Clev.	.270	100	304	48	82	20	67	2
Jones, Lynn, Det.	.296	95	213	33	63	4	26	9
Jones, Ruppert, Sea.*	.267	162	622	109	166	21	78	33
Kemp, Steve, Det.*	.318	134	490	88	156	26	105	5
Kuiper, Duane, Clev.*	.255	140	479	46	122	0	39	4
La Cock, Pete, K.C.*	.277	132	408	54	113	3	56	2
Landreaux, Ken, Minn.*	.305	151	564	81	172	15	83	10
Lansford, Carney, Calif.	.287	157	654	114	188	19	79	20
LeFlore, Ron, Det.	.300	148	600	110	180	9	57	78
Lemon, Chet, Chi.	.318	148	556	79	177	17	86	7
Lezcano, Sixto, Milw.	.321	138	473	84	152	28	101	4
Lowenstein, John, Balt.*	.254	97	197	33	50	11	34	16
Lynn, Fred, Bos.*	.333	147	531	116	177	39	122	2
Manning, Rick, Clev.*	.259	144	560	67	145	3	51	30
Martinez, Buck, Milw.	.270	69	196	17	53	4	26	0
May, Lee, Balt.	.254	124	456	59	116	19	69	3
May, Milt,								
6-Det. 65-Chi.*	.254	71	213	24	54	7	31	0
Mayberry, John, Tor.*	.274	137	464	61	127	21	74	1
McRae, Hal, K.C.	.288	101	393	55	113	10	74	5
Mendoza, Mario, Sea.	.198	148	373	26	74	1	29	3
Meyer, Dan, Sea.*	.278	144	525	72	146	20	74	11
Milbourne, Larry, Sea.†	.278	123	356	40	99	2	26	5
Miller, Rick, Calif.*	.293	120	427	60	125	2	28	5
Molitor, Paul, Milw.	.322	140	584	88	188	9	62	33
Money, Don, Milw.	.237	92	350	52	83	6	38	1
Moore, Alvin, Chi.	.264	88	201	24	53	1	23	0
Moore, Charlie, Milw.	.300	111	337	45	101	5	38	8
Morales, Jerry, Det.	.211	129	440	50	93	14	56	10
Morales, Jose, Minn.	.267	92	191	21	51	2	27	0
Morrison, Jim, Chi.	.275	67	240	38	66	14	35	11
Munson, Thurman, N.Y.	.288	97	382	42	110	3	39	1
Murcer, Bobby, N.Y.*	.273	74	264	42	72	8	33	1
Murphy, Dwayne, Oak.*	.255	121	388	57	99	11	40	15

Batter, Club	PCT	G	AB	R	H	HR	RBI	SB
Murray, Eddie, Balt.†	.295	159	606	90	179	25	99	10
Murray, Larry, Oak.†	.186	105	226	25	42	2	20	6
Nahorodny, Bill, Chi.	.257	65	179	20	46	6	29	0
Nettles, Graig, N.Y.*	.253	145	521	71	132	20	73	1
Newman, Jeff, Oak.	.231	143	516	53	119	22	71	2
Nordhagen, Wayne, Chi.	.280	78	193	20	54	7	25	0
Norman, Nelson, Tex.†	.222	147	343	36	76	0	21	4
Norris, Jim, Clev.*	.246	124	353	50	87	3	30	15
Norwood, Willie, Minn.	.248	98	270	32	67	6	30	9
Oglivie, Ben, Milw.*	.282	139	514	88	145	29	81	12
Oliver, Al, Tex.*	.323	136	492	69	159	12	76	4
Orta, Jorge, Chi.*	.262	113	325	49	85	11	46	1
Otis, Amos, K.C.	.295	151	577	100	170	18	90	30
Paciorek, Tom, Sea.	.287	103	310	38	89	6	42	6
Page, Mitchell, Oak.*	.247	133	478	51	118	9	42	17
Parrish, Lance, Det.	.276	143	493	65	136	19	65	6
Patek, Fred, K.C.	.252	106	306	30	77	1	37	11
Picciolo, Rob, Oak.	.253	115	348	37	88	2	27	2
Piniella, Lou, N.Y.	.297	130	461	49	137	11	69	3
Poquette, Tom, 21-K.C. 63-Bos.*	.311	84	180	15	56	2	26	2
Porter, Darrell, K.C.*	.291	157	533	101	155	20	112	3
Powell, Hosken, Minn.*	.293	104	338	49	99	2	36	5
Pryor, Greg, Chi.	.275	143	476	60	131	3	34	3
Putnam, Pat, Tex.*	.277	139	426	57	118	18	64	1
Randall, Bob, Minn.	.246	80	199	25	49	0	14	2
Randolph, Willie, N.Y.	.270	153	574	98	155	5	61	32
Remy, Jerry, Bos.*	.297	80	306	49	91	0	29	14
Revering, Dave, Oak.*	.288	125	472	63	136	19	77	1
Rice, Jim, Bos.	.325	158	619	117	201	39	130	9
Rivera, Bombo, Minn.	.281	112	263	37	74	2	31	5
Rivers, Mickey, 74-N.Y. 58-Tex.*	.293	132	533	72	156	9	50	10
Roberts, Leon, Sea.	.271	140	450	61	122	15	54	3
Rodriguez, Aurelio, Det.	.254	106	343	27	87	5	36	0
Roenicke, Gary, Balt.	.261	133	376	60	98	25	64	1
Rudi, Joe, Calif.	.242	90	330	35	80	11	61	0
Sample, Bill, Tex.	.292	128	325	60	95	5	35	8
Scott, George, 45-Bos. 44-K.C. 16-N.Y.	.254	105	346	46	88	6	49	2

Batter, Club	PCT	G	AB	R	H	HR	RBI	SB
Simpson, Joe, Sea.*	.283	120	265	29	75	2	27	6
Singleton, Ken, Balt.†	.295	159	570	93	168	35	111	3
Smalley, Roy, Minn.†	.271	162	621	94	168	24	95	2
Smith, Billy, Balt.†	.249	68	189	18	47	6	33	1
Soderholm, Eric, 56-Chi. 63-Tex.	.261	119	357	46	93	10	53	0
Spencer, Jim, N.Y.*	.288	106	295	60	85	23	53	0
Squires, Mike, Chi.*	.264	122	295	44	78	2	22	15
Staub, Rusty, Det.*	.236	68	246	32	58	9	40	1
Stein, Bill, Sea.	.248	88	250	28	62	7	27	1
Stinson, Bob, Sea.†	.243	95	247	19	60	6	28	1
Summers, Champ, Det.*	.313	90	246	47	77	20	51	7
Sundberg, Jim, Tex.	.275	150	495	50	136	5	64	3
Thomas, Gorman, Milw.	.244	156	557	97	136	45	123	1
Thompson, Jason, Det.*	.246	145	492	58	121	20	79	2
Thornton, Andre, Clev.	.233	143	515	89	120	26	93	5
Trammell, Alan, Det.	.276	142	460	68	127	6	50	17
Velez, Otto, Tor.	.288	99	274	45	79	15	48	0
Veryzer, Tom, Clev.	.220	149	449	41	99	0	34	2
Washington, Claudell, Chi.*	.280	131	471	79	132	13	66	19
Washington, U.L., K.C.†	.254	101	268	32	68	2	25	10
Wathan, John, K.C.	.206	90	199	26	41	2	28	2
Watson, Bob, Bos.	.337	84	312	48	105	13	53	3
Whitaker, Lou, Det.*	.286	127	423	75	121	3	42	20
White, Frank, K.C.	.266	127	467	73	124	10	48	28
White, Roy, N.Y.†	.215	81	205	24	44	3	27	2
Wilfong, Rob, Minn.*	.313	140	419	71	131	9	59	11
Wills, Bump, Tex.†	.273	146	543	90	148	5	46	35
Wilson, Willie, K.C.†	.315	154	588	113	185	6	49	83
Wockenfuss, John, Det.	.264	87	231	27	61	15	46	2
Wohlford, Jim, Milw.	.263	63	175	19	46	1	17	6
Woods, Al, Tor.*	.278	132	436	57	121	5	36	6
Wynegar, Butch, Minn.†	.270	149	504	74	136	7	57	2
Yastrzemski, Carl, Bos.*	.270	147	518	69	140	21	87	3
Yount, Robin, Milw.	.267	149	577	72	154	8	51	11
Zisk, Richie, Tex.	.262	144	503	69	132	18	64	1

NATIONAL LEAGUE
Batting
(85 or more at-bats)
*Bats Left-handed †Switch-Hitter

Batter and Club	PCT	G	AB	R	H	HR	RBI	SB
Almon, William, S.D.	.227	100	198	20	45	1	8	6
Andrews, Robert, S.F.	.260	75	154	22	40	2	13	4
Ashby, Alan, Hou.†	.202	108	336	25	68	2	35	0
Auerbach, Frederick, Cin.	.210	62	100	17	21	1	12	0
Baker, Johnnie, L.A.	.274	151	554	86	152	23	88	11
Benedict, Bruce, Atl.	.225	76	204	14	46	0	15	1
Bevacqua, Kurt, S.D.	.253	114	297	23	75	1	34	2
Biittner, Larry, Chi.*	.290	111	272	35	79	3	50	1
Blackwell, Timothy, Chi.†	.164	63	122	8	20	0	12	0
Blair, Paul, Cin.	.150	75	140	7	21	2	15	0
Bochy, Bruce, Hou.	.217	56	129	11	28	1	6	0
Boisclair, Bruce, N.Y.*	.184	59	98	7	18	0	4	0
Bonnell, R. Barry, Atl.	.259	127	375	47	97	12	45	8
Boone, Robert, Phil.	.286	119	398	38	114	9	58	1
Bowa, Lawrence, Phil.†	.241	147	539	74	130	0	31	20
Briggs, Daniel, S.D.*	.207	104	227	34	47	8	30	2
Brock, Louis, St. L.*	.304	120	405	56	123	5	38	21
Buckner, William, Chi.*	.284	149	591	72	168	14	66	9
Burroughs, Jeffrey, Atl.	.224	116	397	49	89	11	47	2
Cabell, Enos, Hou.	.272	155	603	60	164	6	67	37
Cardenal, Jose, Phil.-N.Y.	.247	40	85	12	21	2	13	2
Carlton, Steven, Phil.*	.223	36	94	9	21	0	10	1
Carter, Gary, Mtl.	.283	141	505	74	143	22	75	3
Cash, David, Mtl.	.321	76	187	24	60	2	19	7
Cedeno, Cesar, Hou.	.262	132	470	57	123	6	54	30
Cey, Ronald, L.A.	.281	150	487	77	137	28	81	3
Chaney, Darrel, Atl.†	.162	63	117	15	19	0	10	2
Clark, Jack, S.F.	.273	143	527	84	144	26	86	11
Clines, Eugene, Chi.	.200	10	10	0	2	0	0	0
Collins, David, Cin.†	.318	122	396	59	126	3	35	16
Concepcion, David, Cin.	.281	149	590	91	166	16	84	19
Correll, Victor, Cin.	.233	48	133	14	31	1	15	0
Cromartie, Warren, Mtl.*	.275	158	659	84	181	8	46	8
Cruz, Hector, S.F.-Cin.	.227	90	207	26	47	4	28	0
Cruz, Jose, Hou.*	.289	157	558	73	161	9	72	36

Player & Club	PCT	G	AB	R	H	HR	RBI	SB
Dade, L. Paul, S.D.	.276	76	283	38	78	1	19	13
Dawson, Andre, Mtl.	.275	155	639	90	176	25	92	35
DeJesus, Ivan, Chi.	.283	160	636	92	180	5	52	24
Dillard, Stephen, Chi.	.283	89	166	31	47	5	24	1
Driessen, Daniel, Cin.*	.250	150	515	72	129	18	75	11
Evans, Barry, S.D.	.216	56	162	9	35	1	14	0
Evans, Darrell, S.F.*	.253	160	562	68	142	17	70	6
Fahey, William, S.D.*	.287	73	209	14	60	3	19	1
Ferguson, Joe, L.A.	.262	122	363	54	95	20	69	1
Flores, Gilberto, N.Y.	.194	70	93	9	18	1	10	2
Flynn, R. Douglas, N.Y.	.243	157	555	35	135	4	61	0
Foli, Timothy, N.Y.-Pitt.	.288	136	532	70	153	1	65	6
Foote, Barry, Chi.	.254	132	429	47	109	16	56	5
Foster, George, Cin.	.302	121	440	68	133	30	98	0
Frias, Jesus, Atl.†	.259	140	475	41	123	1	44	3
Garner, Philip, Pitt.	.293	150	549	76	161	11	59	17
Garvey, Steven, L.A.	.315	162	648	92	204	28	110	3
Geronimo, Cesar, Cin.*	.239	123	356	38	85	4	38	1
Gonzalez, J. Fernando, S.D.	217	114	323	22	70	9	34	0
Gonzalez, Julio, Hou.	.249	68	181	16	45	0	10	2
Griffey, G. Kenneth, Cin.*	.316	95	380	62	120	8	32	12
Gross, Gregory, Phil.*	.333	111	174	21	58	0	15	5
Hargrove, D. Michael, S.D.*	192	52	125	15	24	0	8	0
Hatcher, Mickey, L.A.	.269	33	93	9	25	1	5	1
Hebner, Richard, N.Y.*	.268	136	473	54	127	10	79	3
Henderson, Kenneth, Cin.-Chi.†	.234	72	94	12	22	2	10	0
Henderson, Stephen, N.Y.	.306	98	350	42	107	5	39	13
Hendrick, George, St. L.	.300	140	493	67	148	16	75	2
Hernandez, Keith, St. L.*	.344	161	610	116	210	11	105	11
Herndon, Larry, S.F.	.257	132	354	35	91	7	36	8
Hill, Marc, S.F.	.207	63	169	20	35	3	15	0
Hodges, Ronald, N.Y.*	.163	59	86	4	14	0	5	0
Horner, J. Robert, Atl.	.314	121	487	66	153	33	98	0
Howe, Arthur, Hou.	.248	118	355	32	88	6	33	3
Hubbard, Glenn, Atl.	.231	97	325	34	75	3	29	0
Iorg, Dane, St.L.*	.291	79	179	12	52	1	21	1
Ivie, Michael, S.F.	.286	133	402	58	115	27	89	5
Johnstone, John, S.D.*	.294	75	201	10	59	0	32	1
Jones, Randall, S.D.	.174	41	86	8	15	0	5	1

Player & Club	PCT	G	AB	R	H	HR	RBI	SB
Joshua, Von, L.A.*	.282	94	142	22	40	3	14	1
Kelleher, Michael, Chi.	.254	73	142	14	36	0	10	2
Kendall, Fred, S.D.	.167	46	102	8	17	1	6	0
Kennedy, Junior, Cin.	.273	83	220	29	60	1	17	4
Kennedy, Terrence, St.L.*	.284	33	109	11	31	2	17	0
Kingman, David, Chi.	.288	145	532	97	153	48	115	4
Knight, C. Ray, Cin.	.318	150	551	64	175	10	79	4
Kranepool, Edward, N.Y.*	.232	82	155	7	36	2	17	0
Lacy, Leondaus, Pitt.	.247	84	182	17	45	5	15	6
Landestoy, Rafael, Hou.†	.270	129	282	33	76	0	30	13
LeMaster, Johnnie, S.F.	.254	108	343	42	87	3	29	9
Leonard, Jeffrey, Hou.	.290	134	411	47	119	0	47	23
Littlejohn, Dennis, S.F.	.197	63	193	15	38	1	13	0
Lopes, David, L.A.	.265	153	582	109	154	28	73	44
Lum, Michael, Atl.*	.249	111	217	27	54	6	27	0
Luzinski, Gregory, Phil.	.252	137	452	47	114	18	81	3
Maddox, Elliott, N.Y.	.268	86	224	21	60	1	12	3
Maddox, Garry, Phil.	.281	148	548	70	154	13	61	26
Madlock, Bill, S.F.-Pitt.	.298	154	560	85	167	14	85	32
Martin, Jerry, Chi.	.272	150	534	74	145	19	73	2
Martinez, Teodoro, L.A.	.268	81	112	19	30	0	2	3
Matthews, Gary, Atl.	.304	156	631	97	192	27	90	18
Mazzilli, Lee, N.Y.†	.303	158	597	78	181	15	79	34
McBride, Arnold, Phil.*	.280	151	582	82	163	12	60	25
McCarver, J. Timothy, Phil.*	.241	79	137	13	33	1	12	2
McCovey, Willie, S.F.*	.249	117	353	34	88	15	57	0
Metzger, Roger, S.F.†	.251	94	259	24	65	0	31	11
Miller, Edward, Atl.†	.310	27	113	12	35	0	5	15
Milner, John, Pitt.*	.276	128	326	52	90	16	60	3
Montanez, Guillermo, N.Y.*	.234	109	410	36	96	5	47	0
Moreno, Omar, Pitt.*	.282	162	695	110	196	8	69	77
Morgan, Joe, Cin.*	.250	127	436	70	109	9	32	28
Mumphrey, Jerry, St.L.†	.295	124	339	53	100	3	32	8
Murcer, Bobby, Chi.*	.258	58	190	22	49	7	22	2
Murphy, Dale, Atl.	.276	104	384	53	106	21	57	6
Nicosia, Steven, Pitt.	.288	70	191	22	55	4	13	0
Niekro, Philip, Atl.	.195	44	123	10	24	0	12	0
Nolan, Joseph, Atl.*	.248	89	230	28	57	4	21	1
Norman, Daniel, N.Y.	.245	44	110	9	27	3	11	2
North, William, S.F.†	.259	142	460	87	119	5	30	58

Player & Club	PCT	G	AB	R	H	HR	RBI	SB
Oberkfell, Kenneth, St.L.*	.301	135	369	53	111	1	35	4
Office, Rowland, Atl.*	.249	124	277	35	69	2	37	5
Ontiveros, Steven, Chi.†	.285	152	519	58	148	4	57	0
Ott, N. Edward, Pitt.*	.273	117	403	49	110	7	51	0
Parker, David, Pitt.*	.310	158	622	109	193	25	94	20
Parrish, Larry, Mtl.	.307	153	544	83	167	30	82	5
Perez, Atanasio, Mtl.	.270	132	489	58	132	13	73	2
Perkins, Broderick, S.D.*	.264	57	87	8	23	0	8	0
Phillips, Michael, St.L.*	.227	44	97	10	22	1	6	0
Puhl, Terry, Hou.*	.287	157	600	87	172	8	49	30
Reitz, Kenneth, St.L.	.268	159	605	42	162	8	73	1
Reynolds, G. Craig, Hou.*	.265	146	555	63	147	0	39	12
Richard, James, Hou.	.126	38	95	6	12	2	6	0
Richards, Eugene, S.D.*	.279	150	545	77	152	4	41	24
Robinson, William, Pitt.	.264	148	421	59	111	24	75	13
Rose, Peter, Phil.†	.331	163	628	90	208	4	59	20
Royster, Jeron, Atl.	.273	154	601	103	164	3	51	35
Russell, William, L.A.	.271	153	627	72	170	7	56	6
Sadek, Michael, S.F.	.238	63	126	14	30	1	11	1
Schmidt, Michael, Phil.	.253	160	541	109	137	45	114	9
Scott, Anthony, St.L.†	.259	153	587	69	152	6	68	37
Scott, Rodney, Mtl.†	.238	151	562	69	134	3	42	39
Simmons, Ted, St.L.†	.283	123	448	68	127	26	87	0
Sizemore, Ted, Chi.	.248	98	330	36	82	2	24	3
Smith, C. Reginald, L.A.†	.274	68	234	41	64	10	32	6
Smith, Osborne, S.D.†	.211	156	587	77	124	0	27	28
Speier, Chris, Mtl.	.227	113	344	31	78	7	26	0
Spikes, L. Charles, Atl.	.280	66	93	12	26	3	21	0
Stargell, Wilver, Pitt.*	.281	126	424	60	119	32	82	0
Staub, Daniel, Mtl.*	.267	38	86	9	23	3	14	0
Stearns, John, N.Y.	.243	155	538	58	131	9	66	15
Stennett, Renaldo, Pitt.	.238	108	319	31	76	0	24	1
Strain, Joseph, S.F.	.241	67	257	27	62	1	12	8
Sutcliffe, Richard, L.A.*	.247	40	85	6	21	1	17	0
Taveras, Franklin, Pitt.-N.Y.	.262	164	680	93	178	1	34	44
Templeton, Garry, St.L.†	.314	154	672	105	211	9	62	26
Tenace, F. Gene, S.D.	.263	151	463	61	122	20	67	2
Thomas, Derrel, L.A.†	.256	141	406	47	104	5	44	18
Thomasson, Gary, L.A.*	.248	115	315	39	78	14	45	4
Thompson, V. Scot, Chi.*	.289	128	346	36	100	2	29	4

Player & Club	PCT	G	AB	R	H	HR	RBI	SB
Trevino, Alejandro, N.Y.	.271	79	207	24	56	0	20	2
Trillo, J. Manuel, Phil.	.260	118	431	40	112	6	42	4
Turner, John, S.D.*	.248	138	448	55	111	9	61	4
Tyson, Michael, St.L.	.221	75	190	18	42	5	20	2
Unser, Delbert, Phil.*	.298	95	141	26	42	6	29	2
Vail, Michael, Chi.	.335	87	179	28	60	7	35	0
Valentine, Ellis, Mtl.	.276	146	548	73	151	21	82	11
Venable, W. McKinley, S.F.*	.165	55	85	12	14	0	3	3
Walling, Dennis, Hou.*	.327	82	147	21	48	3	31	3
Watson, Robert, Hou.	.239	49	163	15	39	3	18	0
White, Jerome, Mtl.†	.297	88	138	30	41	3	18	8
Whitfield, Terry, S.F.*	.287	133	394	52	113	5	44	5
Wilhelm, James, S.D.	.243	39	103	8	25	0	8	1
Winfield, David, S.D.	.308	159	597	97	184	34	118	15
Yeager, Stephen, L.A.	.216	105	310	33	67	13	41	1
Youngblood, Joel, N.Y.	.275	158	590	90	162	16	60	18

1979 STATISTICS
AMERICAN LEAGUE
Pitching
(75 or more innings)
*Pitches Left-handed

Pitcher and Club	ERA	W	L	G	IP	H	BB	SO
Aase, Don, Calif.	4.82	9	10	37	185	200	77	96
Abbott, Glenn, Sea.	5.15	4	10	23	117	138	38	25
Alexander, Doyle, Tex.	4.46	5	7	23	113	114	69	50
Augustine, Jerry, Milw.*	3.45	9	6	43	86	95	30	41
Baker, Steve, Det.	6.64	1	7	21	84	97	51	54
Bannister, Floyd, Sea.*	4.05	10	15	30	182	185	68	115
Barker, Len, Clev.	4.93	6	6	29	137	146	70	93
Barlow, Mike, Calif.	5.13	1	1	35	86	106	30	33
Barr, Jim, Calif.	4.20	10	12	36	197	217	55	69
Barrios, Francisco, Chi.	3.60	8	3	15	95	88	33	28
Baumgarten, Ross, Chi.*	3.53	13	8	28	191	175	83	72
Beattie, Jim, N.Y.	5.21	3	6	15	76	85	41	32
Billingham, Jack, Det.	3.30	10	7	35	158	163	60	59
Burgmeier, Tom, Bos.*	2.73	3	2	44	89	89	16	60
Busby, Steve, K.C.	3.64	6	6	22	94	71	64	45
Buskey, Tom, Tor.	3.42	6	10	44	79	74	25	44
Caldwell, Mike, Milw.*	3.29	16	6	30	235	252	39	89
Chamberlain, Craig, K.C.	3.73	4	4	10	70	68	18	30
Clay, Ken, N.Y.	5.42	1	7	32	78	88	25	28
Clear, Mark, Calif.	3.63	11	5	52	109	87	68	98
Comer, Steve, Tex.	3.68	17	12	36	242	230	84	86
Cruz, Victor, Clev.	4.22	3	9	61	79	70	44	63
Darwin, Danny, Tex.	4.04	4	4	20	78	50	30	58
Davis, Ron, N.Y.	2.86	14	2	44	85	84	28	43
Drago, Dick, Bos.	3.03	10	6	53	89	85	21	67
Dressler, Rob, Sea.	4.93	3	2	21	104	134	22	36
Eckersley, Dennis, Bos.	2.99	17	10	33	247	234	59	150
Erickson, Roger, Minn.	5.63	3	10	24	123	154	48	47
Farmer, Ed, 11-Tex. 42-Chi.	3.00	5	7	53	114	96	53	73
Figueroa, Ed, N.Y.	4.11	4	6	16	105	109	35	42
Flanagan, Mike, Balt.*	3.08	23	9	39	266	245	70	190
Freisleben, Dave, Tor.	4.95	2	3	42	91	101	54	35

Pitcher and Club	ERA	W	L	G	IP	H	BB	SO
Frost, Dave, Calif.	3.58	16	10	36	239	226	77	107
Gale, Rich, K.C.	5.64	9	10	34	182	197	99	103
Garland, Wayne, Clev.	5.21	4	10	18	95	120	34	40
Goltz, Dave, Minn.	4.16	14	13	36	251	282	69	132
Guidry, Ron, N.Y.*	2.78	18	8	33	236	203	71	201
Gura, Larry, K.C.*	4.46	13	12	39	234	226	73	85
Haas, Moose, Milw.	4.77	11	11	29	185	198	59	95
Hamilton, Dave, Oak.*	3.69	3	4	40	83	80	43	52
Hartzell, Paul, Minn.	5.36	6	10	28	163	193	44	44
Heaverlo, Dave, Oak.	4.08	4	11	62	86	97	42	40
Hiller, John, Det.*	5.24	4	7	43	79	83	55	46
Honeycutt, Rick, Sea.*	4.04	11	12	33	194	201	67	83
Hood, Don,								
13-Clev. 27-N.Y.*	3.24	4	1	40	89	75	44	29
Huffman, Phil, Tor.	5.77	6	18	31	173	220	68	56
Hunter, Catfish, N.Y.	5.31	2	9	19	105	128	34	34
Jefferson, Jesse, Tor.	5.51	2	10	34	116	150	45	43
Jenkins, Ferguson, Tex.	4.07	16	14	37	259	252	81	164
John, Tommy, N.Y.*	2.97	21	9	37	276	268	65	111
Johnson, John,								
14-Oak. 17-Tex.*	4.63	4	14	31	167	168	72	96
Jones, Odell, Sea.	6.05	3	11	25	119	151	58	72
Keough, Matt, Oak.	5.03	2	17	30	177	220	78	95
Kern, Jim, Tex.	1.57	13	5	71	143	99	62	136
Kingman, Brian, Oak.	4.30	8	7	18	113	113	33	59
Knapp, Chris, Calif.	5.51	5	5	20	98	109	35	36
Koosman, Jerry, Minn.*	3.38	20	13	37	264	268	83	157
Kravec, Ken, Chi.*	3.74	15	13	36	250	208	111	132
Langford, Rick, Oak.	4.27	12	16	34	219	233	57	101
LaRoche, Dave, Calif.*	5.55	7	11	53	86	107	32	59
Lemanczyk, Dave, Tor.	3.71	8	10	22	143	137	45	63
Lemongello, Mark, Tor.	6.29	1	9	18	83	97	34	40
Leonard, Dennis, K.C.	4.08	14	12	32	236	226	56	126
Luebber, Steve, Tor.	Inf.	0	0	1	0	2	1	0
Lyle, Sparky, Tex.*	3.13	5	8	67	95	78	28	48
Marshall, Mike, Minn.	2.64	10	15	90	143	132	48	81
Martinez, Dennis, Balt.	3.67	15	16	40	292	279	78	132
Martinez, Tippy, Balt.*	2.88	10	3	39	78	59	31	61
Matlack, Jon, Tex.*	4.13	5	4	13	85	98	15	35
McCatty, Steve, Oak.	4.21	11	12	31	186	207	80	87

Pitcher and Club	ERA	W	L	G	IP	H	BB	SO
McGregor, Scott, Balt.*	3.34	13	6	27	175	165	23	81
McLaughlin, Byron, Sea.	4.21	7	7	47	124	114	60	74
Medich, Doc, Tex.	4.17	10	7	29	149	156	49	58
Minetto, Craig, Oak.*	5.57	1	5	36	118	131	58	64
Mitchell, Paul, 10-Sea. 18-Milw.	5.30	4	7	28	112	127	25	50
Monge, Sid, Clev.*	2.40	12	10	76	131	96	64	108
Montague, John, 41-Sea. 14-Calif.	5.51	8	4	55	134	141	56	66
Moore, Balor, Tor.*	4.86	5	7	34	139	135	79	51
Morgan, Mike, Oak.	5.96	2	10	13	77	102	50	17
Morris, Jack, Det.	3.27	17	7	27	198	179	59	113
Norris, Mike, Oak.	4.81	5	8	29	146	146	94	96
Palmer, Jim, Balt.	3.29	10	6	23	156	144	43	67
Parrott, Mike, Sea.	3.77	14	12	38	229	231	86	127
Pattin, Marty, K.C.	4.60	5	2	31	94	109	21	41
Paxton, Mike, Clev.	5.91	8	8	33	160	210	52	70
Petry, Dan, Det.	3.95	6	5	15	98	90	33	43
Proly, Mike, Chi.	3.89	3	8	38	88	89	40	32
Rainey, Chuck, Bos.	3.81	8	5	20	104	97	41	41
Rawley, Shane, Sea.*	3.86	5	9	48	84	88	40	48
Redfern, Pete, Minn.	3.50	7	3	40	108	106	35	85
Renko, Steve, Bos.	4.11	11	9	27	171	174	58	99
Rodriguez, Ed, K.C.	4.86	4	1	29	74	79	34	26
Rozema, Dave, Det.	3.53	4	4	16	97	101	30	33
Ryan, Nolan, Calif.	3.59	16	14	34	223	169	114	223
Scarbery, Randy, Chi.	4.63	2	8	45	101	102	34	45
Slaton, Jim, Milw.	3.63	15	9	32	213	229	54	80
Sorensen, Lary, Milw.	3.98	15	14	34	235	250	42	63
Spillner, Dan, Clev.	4.61	9	5	49	158	153	64	97
Splittorff, Paul, K.C.*	4.24	15	17	36	240	248	77	77
Stanhouse, Don, Balt.	2.84	7	3	52	73	49		34
Stanley, Bob, Bos.	3.98	16	12	40	217	250	44	56
Stewart, Sammy, Balt.	3.51	8	5	31	118	96	71	71
Stieb, Dave, Tor.	4.33	8	8	18	129	139	48	52
Stone, Steve, Balt.	3.77	11	7	32	186	173	73	96
Tanana, Frank, Calif.*	3.90	7	5	18	90	93	25	46
Tiant, Luis, N.Y.	3.90	13	8	30	196	190	53	104
Todd, Jim, Oak.	6.44	2	5	51	81	108	51	26
Torrez, Mike, Bos.	4.50	16	13	36	252	254	121	125

Pitcher and Club	ERA	W	L	G	IP	H	BB	SO
Travers, Bill, Milw.*	3.90	14	8	30	187	196	45	74
Trout, Steve, Chi.*	3.89	11	8	34	155	165	59	76
Underwood, Pat, Det.*	4.57	6	4	27	122	126	29	83
Underwood, Tom, Tor.*	3.69	9	16	33	227	213	95	127
Waits, Rick, Clev.*	4.44	16	13	34	231	230	91	91
Wilcox, Milt, Det.	4.36	12	10	33	196	201	73	109
Wilkins, Eric, Clev.	4.37	2	4	16	70	77	38	52
Wise, Rick, Clev.	3.72	15	10	34	232	229	68	108
Wortham, Rich, Chi.*	4.90	14	14	34	204	195	100	119
Zahn, Geoff, Minn.*	3.57	13	7	26	169	181	41	58

NATIONAL LEAGUE

Pitching
(80 or more innings)
*Pitches Left-handed

Pitcher and Club	ERA	W	L	G	IP	H	BB	SO
Allen, Neil, N.Y.	3.55	6	10	50	99	100	47	65
Andujar, Joaquin, Hou.	3.43	12	12	46	194	168	88	77
Bahnsen, Stanley, Mtl.	3.16	3	1	55	94	80	42	71
Bair, C. Douglas, Cin.	4.31	11	7	65	94	93	51	86
Bibby, James, Pitt.	2.80	12	4	34	138	110	47	103
Blue, Vida, S.F.*	5.01	14	14	34	237	246	111	138
Blyleven, R. Aalbert, Pitt.	3.61	12	5	37	237	238	92	172
Bonham, William, Cin.	3.78	9	7	29	176	173	60	78
Borbon, Pedro, Cin.-S.F.	4.15	6	5	60	91	104	21	49
Brizzolara, Anthony, Atl.	5.30	6	9	20	107	133	33	64
Candelaria, John, Pitt.*	3.22	14	9	33	207	201	41	101
Carlton, Steven, Phil.*	3.62	18	11	35	251	202	89	213
Caudill, William, Chi.	4.80	1	7	29	90	89	41	104
Coleman, Joseph, S.F.-Pitt.	5.25	0	0	15	24	32	11	14
Curtis, John, S.F.*	4.17	10	9	27	121	121	42	85
D'Acquisto, John, S.D.	4.90	9	13	51	134	140	86	97
Denny, John, St. L.	4.85	8	11	31	206	206	100	99
Eastwick, Rawlins, Phil.	4.88	3	6	51	83	90	25	47
Ellis, Dock, N.Y.-Pitt.	5.77	3	7	20	92	119	36	42
Espinosa, Arnulfo, Phil.	3.65	14	12	33	212	211	65	88
Falcone, Peter, N.Y.*	4.16	6	14	33	184	194	76	113
Fingers, Roland, S.D.	4.50	9	9	54	84	91	37	65

Pitcher and Club	ERA	W	L	G	IP	H	BB	SO
Forsch, Kenneth, Hou.	3.03	11	6	26	178	155	35	58
Forsch, Robert, St. L.	3.82	11	11	33	219	215	52	92
Fulgham, John, St. L.	2.53	10	6	20	146	123	26	75
Garber, H. Eugene, Atl.	4.33	6	16	68	106	121	24	56
Griffin, Thomas, S.F.	3.93	5	6	59	94	83	46	82
Grimsley, Ross, Mtl.*	5.36	10	9	32	151	199	41	42
Halicki, Edward, S.F.	4.57	5	8	33	126	134	47	81
Holtzman, Kenneth, Chi.*	4.58	6	9	23	118	133	53	44
Hooton, Burt, L.A.	2.97	11	10	29	212	191	63	129
Hough, Charles, L.A.	4.77	7	5	42	151	152	66	76
Hume, Thomas, Cin.	2.76	10	9	57	163	162	33	80
Jones, Randall, S.D.*	3.63	11	12	39	263	257	64	112
Kison, Bruce, Pitt.	3.19	13	7	33	172	157	45	105
Knepper, Robert, S.F.*	4.65	9	12	34	207	241	77	123
Kobel, Kevin, N.Y.*	3.50	6	8	30	162	169	46	67
Krukow, Michael, Chi.	4.20	9	9	28	165	172	81	119
LaCoss, Michael, Cin.	3.50	14	8	35	206	202	79	73
Lamp, Dennis, Chi.	3.51	11	10	38	200	223	46	86
Lavelle, Gary, S.F.*	2.51	7	9	70	97	86	42	80
Lee, William, Mtl.*	3.04	16	10	33	222	230	46	59
Lerch, Randy, Phil.*	3.74	10	13	37	214	228	60	92
Littell, Mark, St.L.	2.20	9	4	63	82	60	39	67
Mahler, Michael, Atl.*	5.85	5	11	26	100	123	47	71
Martinez, Silvio, St.L.	3.26	15	8	32	207	204	67	102
Matula, Richard, Atl.	4.16	8	10	28	171	193	64	67
May, Rudolph, Mtl.*	2.30	10	3	33	94	88	31	67
McGlothen, Lynn, Chi.	4.12	13	14	42	212	236	55	147
McGraw, Frank, Phil.*	5.14	4	3	65	84	83	29	57
Montefusco, John, S.F.	3.94	3	8	22	137	145	51	76
Moskau, Paul, Cin.	3.91	5	4	21	106	107	51	58
Murray, Dale, N.Y.-Mtl.	4.58	5	10	67	110	119	55	41
Nastu, Philip, S.F.*	4.32	3	4	25	100	105	41	47
Niekro, Joseph, Hou.	3.00	21	11	38	264	221	107	119
Niekro, Philip, Atl.	3.39	21	20	44	342	311	113	208
Noles, Dickie, Phil.	3.80	3	4	14	90	80	38	42
Norman, Fredie, Cin.*	3.65	11	13	34	195	193	57	95
Owchinko, Robert, S.D.*	3.74	6	12	42	149	144	55	66
Palmer, David, Mtl.	2.63	10	2	36	123	110	30	72
Pastore, Frank, Cin.	4.26	6	7	30	95	102	23	63
Perry, Gaylord, S.D.	3.05	12	11	32	233	225	67	140

Pitcher and Club	ERA	W	L	G	IP	H	BB	SO
Rasmussen, Eric, S.D.	3.27	6	9	45	157	142	42	54
Reed, Ronald, Phil.	4.15	13	8	61	102	110	32	58
Reuschel, Ricky, Chi.	3.62	18	12	36	239	251	75	125
Reuss, Jerry, L.A.*	3.54	7	14	39	160	178	60	83
Richard, James, Hou.	2.71	18	13	38	292	220	98	313
Robinson, Don, Pitt.	3.86	8	8	29	161	171	52	96
Rogers, Stephen, Mtl.	3.00	13	12	37	249	232	78	143
Romo, Enrique, Pitt.	3.00	10	5	84	129	122	43	106
Rooker, James, Pitt.*	4.59	4	7	19	104	106	39	44
Ruthven, Richard, Phi.	4.28	7	5	20	122	121	37	58
Sanderson, Scott, Mtl.	3.43	9	8	34	168	148	54	138
Schatzeder, Daniel, Mtl.*	2.83	10	5	32	162	136	59	106
Seaver, G. Thomas, Cin.	3.14	16	6	32	215	187	61	131
Shirley, Robert, S.D.*	3.38	8	16	49	205	196	59	117
Solomon, Eddie, Atl.	4.21	7	14	31	186	184	51	96
Sosa, Elias, Mtl.	1.95	8	7	62	97	77	37	59
Sutcliffe, Richard, L.A.	3.46	17	10	39	242	217	97	117
Sutter, H. Bruce, Chi.	2.23	6	6	62	101	67	32	110
Sutton, Donald, L.A.	3.82	12	15	33	226	201	61	146
Swan, Craig, N.Y.	3.30	14	13	35	251	241	57	145
Tekulve, Kenton, Pitt.	2.75	10	8	94	134	109	49	75
Tidrow, Richard, Chi.	2.71	11	5	63	103	86	42	68
Vuckovich, Peter, St.L.	3.59	15	10	34	233	229	64	145
Whitson, Eddie, Pitt.-S.F.	4.10	7	11	37	158	151	75	93
Williams, Richard, Hou.	3.27	4	7	31	121	122	30	37